Carrying on in Key Stage 1

Water

Published 2011 by A&C Black Publishers Limited
36 Soho Square, London W1D 3QY

www.acblack.com

ISBN 978-1-4081-3976-9

First published 2008 by Featherstone Education Ltd

Text © Ros Bayley, Lyn Broadbent, Sally Featherstone 2008

Photographs © Fotolia 2011, Shutterstock 2011

Additional photos © Lynn Broadbent, Ros Bayley, Sally Featherstone, Sarah
Featherstone 2008, ASCO

Designed by Lynda Murray

A CIP record for this publication is available from the British Library.

Printed in Malta by Gutenburg Press Ltd

This book is produced using paper that is made from wood grown in managed,
sustainable forests. It is natural, renewable and recyclable.

The logging and manufacturing processes conform to the environmental
regulations of the country of origin.

To see our full range of titles visit **www.acblack.com**

Contents

Introduction

This series of books is intended to support the continuing growth and development of independent learning and practical activities, which are key features of the Early Years Foundation Stage (EYFS).

Children in Key Stage 1 need and deserve the chance to build on the best of practice in the EYFS, which carefully balances adult directed tasks with learning that children initiate and develop themselves, often in the company of responsive adults. These activities, which include sand and water play, construction, role play, independent mark making and writing, creative work, dance and movement, and outdoor play, are some of the activities children value most and miss most in Years 1 and 2.

What's it like in year 1?

There en't no sand and the work's too 'ard.

This quote from a Year 1 boy echoes the feelings of many children who need a continuation of the learning styles and situations offered in Reception classes. However, many teachers in Key Stage One feel intense pressure to concentrate on activities that require recording and increasing levels of direction from adults. Why is this, and is it right for teachers to feel so pressured?

One thing we know from research is that practical activity and independent learning are essential for brain growth and reinforcement of growing abilities throughout childhood, at least until the onset of puberty, and for many children this is a lifelong need. We also know that the embedding of learning and the transformation of this into real understanding takes time and practice. Skills need to be reinforced by revisiting them in many different contexts in child-initiated learning and practical

challenges. Practical tasks in real life situations will be far more effective than rote learning, worksheets or adult direction.

It is also clear from brain research that many boys (and some girls) are just not ready by the end of Reception to embark on a formal curriculum which involves a lot of sitting down, listening and writing. Their bodies and their brains still need action, challenge and freedom to explore materials and resources.

But this does not mean that challenge should be absent from such activity! The brain feeds on challenge and novelty, so teachers and other adults working in Key Stage One need to structure the experiences, so they build on existing skills and previous activities, while presenting opportunities to explore familiar materials in new and exciting ways. Such challenges and activities can:

- be led by the Programme of Study for Key Stage 1
- focus on thinking skills and personal capabilities
- relate to real world situations and stimuli
- help children to achieve the five outcomes for Every Child Matters.

'I hear and I forget,
I see and I remember,
I do and I understand.'
Ancient Chinese Proverb

Every Child Matters

The five outcomes:

- Enjoy and achieve
- Stay safe
- Be healthy
- Make a positive contribution
- Achieve economic well-being

In **Carrying on in Key Stage 1**, we aim to give you the rationale, the process and the confidence to continue a practical, child-centred curriculum which also helps you as teachers to meet the requirements of the statutory curriculum for Key Stage One. Each book in the series follows the same format, and addresses objectives from many areas of the National Curriculum. Of course, when children work on practical challenges, curriculum elements become intertwined, and many will be going on simultaneously.

The role of the adult

Of course, even during child-initiated learning, the role of the adult is crucial. Sensitive adults play many roles as they support, challenge and engage the children in their care. High quality teaching is not easy! If teachers want to expand experiences and enhance learning, they need to be able to stand back, to work alongside, and to extend or scaffold the children's learning by offering provocations and challenges to their thinking. The diagram on the right attempts to describe this complex task, and the way that adults move around the elements in the circle of learning. For ease of reading we have described the elements in the following way, and each double page spread covers all three of the vital roles adults play.

Previous experience: recognising and building on the practical activities which children have experienced before

This element of the process is vital in scaffolding children's learning so it makes sense to them. Your knowledge of the Foundation Stage curriculum and the way it is organised will be vital in knowing where to start.

Teachers and other adults should have first hand knowledge of both the resources and the activities which have been available and how they have been offered in both child-initiated and adult-led activities. This knowledge should be gained by visiting the Reception classes in action, and by talking to adults and children as they work. Looking at Reception planning will also help.

The responsive adult: Understanding the range of adult roles, and the effect different roles have on children's learning

Responsive adults react in different ways to what they see and hear during the day. This knowledge will influence the way they plan for further experiences to meet emerging needs and build on individual interests. The diagram illustrates the complex and interlinking ways in which adults interact with children's learning. Observing, co-playing and extending learning often happen simultaneously, flexibly and sometimes unconsciously. It is only when we reflect on our work with children that we realise what a complex and skilled activity is going on.

Offering challenges and provocations

As the adults collect information about the learning, they begin to see how they can help children to extend and scaffold their thinking and learning. The adults offer challenges or provocations which act like grit in an oyster, provoking the children to produce responses and think in new ways about what they know and can do.

Linking the learning with the skills and content of the curriculum

As the children grapple with new concepts and skills, adults can make direct links with curriculum intentions and content. These links can be mapped out across the range of knowledge, skills and understanding contained in the curriculum guidance for Key Stage One. It is also possible to map the development of thinking skills, personal capabilities and concepts which link the taught curriculum with the real world.

The adult as extender of learning
- discusses ideas
- shares thinking
- makes new possibilities evident
- instigates new opportunities for learning
- extends and builds on learning and interests
- supports children in making links in learning
- models new skills and techniques

The adult as co-player
- shares responsibility with the child
- offers suggestions
- asks open questions
- responds sensitively
- models and imitates
- plays alongside

The adult as observer
- listens attentively
- observes carefully
- records professionally
- interprets skilfully

As children plan, explore, invent, extend, construct, discuss, question and predict in the rich experiences planned and offered, they will communicate what they are learning through speech and actions, as well as through the outcomes of activities.

Looking for the learning

Assessment for learning involves adults and children in sharing and analysing what they discover. Reflecting on learning, through discussion with other children and adults, is a key factor in securing skills and abilities, fixing and 'hard wiring' the learning in each child's brain. And, of course, teachers and other adults need to recognise, confirm and record children's achievements, both for the self esteem this brings to the children and to fulfil their own duties as educators.

You could find out what children already know and have experienced by:

- talking to them as individuals and in small groups

- talking to parents and other adults who know them well (teaching assistants are often wonderful sources of information about individual children)

- visiting the Reception classes and looking at spaces, storage and access to resources, including the use of these out of doors

- providing free access to materials and equipment and watching how children use them when you are not giving any guidance

- talking as a group or class about what children already know about the materials and those they particularly enjoy using.

Using the curriculum grid to observe, to recognise learning and celebrate achievement

At the end of this section you will find a photocopiable curriculum grid covering the whole Programme of Study for Key Stage 1 which can be used for planning and particularly for recording observations. This is a 'shorthand version' of the full grid included at the end of the book on pages 40-48.

We suggest that as the children work on the provocations and other challenges in this book, adults (teachers and teaching assistants) can use the grid to observe groups of children and record the areas of the curriculum they are covering in their work. The grid can also be used to record what children say and describe in plenary sessions and other discussions.

These observations will enable you to recognise the learning that happens as children explore the materials and engage with the challenging questions you ask and the problems you pose. And of course, as you observe, you will begin to see what needs to happen next; identifying the next steps in learning! This logical and vital stage in the process may identify:

- some children who will be ready for more of the same activity

- some who need to repeat and reinforce previous stages

- some who need to relate skills to new contexts, the same activity or skill practised in a new place or situation

- some who will want to extend or sustain the current activity in time, space or detail

- others who will wish to record their work in photos, drawings, models, stories, video and so on.

The grid also identifies the key skills which children need for thinking about and evaluating their work. Many schools now observe and evaluate how well these skills are developing when children work on challenging projects and investigations.

Ready for more?

Offering extension activities is a way of scaffolding children's learning, taking the known into the unknown, the familiar into the new, the secure into the challenging. It is the role of the adult to turn their knowledge of the children into worthwhile, long-term lines of enquiry and development which will become self-sustaining and last throughout life.

At the end of each section in the book you will find a selection of useful resources, links and other information to help you support children in making structures, sculptures and other 3D creations. You could use these resources by encouraging individuals and groups:

■ to use the Internet to find images and information

■ to use ICT equipment such as cameras, tape recorders, video and dictaphones to record their explorations and experiments

■ to explore information books in libraries and other places at home and at school

■ to make contact by email and letter with experts, craftsmen, artists, manufacturers, suppliers and other contacts

■ to make books, films, PowerPoint presentations

■ to record their work in photographs and other media

■ to respond to stimuli such as photographs, video, exhibitions and other creative stimuli

■ to look at the built and natural environment with curiosity, interest and creativity

■ to become involved in preserving the natural world, develop environmental awareness and support recycling

■ to look at the world of work and extend their ideas of what they might become and how they might live their lives

■ to develop a sense of economic awareness and the world of work in its widest sense

■ to feel a sense of community and to explore how they might make a contribution to the school and wider communities in which they live

■ to work together and develop the ability to think, reason and solve problems in their learning.

The suggested resources include websites, books, contacts and addresses. There are also some photographs which may inspire young learners as they work on the provocations and challenges suggested.

We hope you will find the ideas in this book useful in stimulating your work with children in Year 1 and Year 2. Before trying the activities please check for allergies and be aware of safety at all times. The ideas, photos and provocations we have included are only a start to your thinking and exploring together. Of course you and the children will have many more as you start to expand the work they do in these practical areas, providing a rich curriculum base using familiar and well loved materiaals.

We recommend that younger children should always work with an adult when accessing search engines and Internet sites.

Planning and observation of _____ (the activity)   Name: _____   Date: _____

Literacy

Lit 1 Speak	Lit 2 Listen	Lit 3 Group	Lit 4 Drama	Lit 5 Word	Lit 6 Spell	Lit 7 Text 1	Lit 8 Text 2	Lit 9 Text 3	Lit 10 Text 4	Lit 11 Sentence	Lit 12 Presentation
1.1	2.1	3.1	4.1	5.1	6.1	7.1	8.1	9.1	10.1	11.1	12.1
1.2	2.2	3.2	4.2	5.2	6.2	7.2	8.2	9.2	10.2	11.2	12.2

Numeracy

Num 1 U&A	Num 2 Count	Num 3 Number	Num 4 Calculate	Num 5 Shape	Num 6 Measure	Num 7 Data
1.1	2.1	3.1	4.1	5.1	6.1	7.1
1.2	2.2	3.2	4.2	5.2	6.2	7.2

Science

SC1 Enquiry			SC2 Life processes					SC3 Materials		SC4 Physical processes		
Sc 1.1	Sc 1.2	Sc 1.3	Sc 2.1	Sc 2.2	Sc 2.3	Sc 2.4	Sc 2.5	Sc 3.1	Sc 3.2	Sc 4.1	Sc4.2	Sc 4.3
1.1a	1.2a	1.3a	2.1a	2.2a	2.3a	2.4a	2,5a	3.1a	3.2a	4.1a	4.2a	4.3a
1.1b	1.2b	1.3b	2.1b	2.2b	2.3b	2.4b	2,5b	3.1b	3.2b	4.1b	4.2b	4.3b
1.1c	1.2c	1.3c	2.1c	2.2c	2.3c		2,5c	3.1c		4.1c	4.2c	4.3c
1.1d				2.2d				3.1d				4.3d
				2.2e								
				2.2f								
				2.2g								

Notes on how to take the learning forward

History

H1 Chronology	H2 Events, people	H3 Interpret	H4 Enquire	H5 Org and comm	H6 Breadth
1a	2a	3a	4a	5a	6a
1b	2b		4b		6b
				6c	
				6d	

Geography

G1.1 and Enquiry	G1.2 Enquiry	G2 Places	G3 Processes	G4 Environment	G5 Breadth
1.1a	1.2a	2a	3a	4a	5a
1.1b	1.2b	2b	3b	4b	5b
1.1c	1.2c	2c			5c
1.1d	1.2d	2d			5d
		2e			

Music

M1 Performing	M2 Composing	M3 Appraising	M4 Listening	M5 Breadth
1a	2a	3a	4a	5a
1b	2b	3b	4b	5b
1c			4c	5c
			5d	

Art and Design

A&D 1 Ideas	A&D 2 Making	A&D 3 Evaluating	A&D 4 Materials	A&D 5 Breadth
1a	2a	3a	4a	5a
1b	2b	3b	4b	5b
	2c		4c	5c
				5d

Design and Technology

D&T 1 Developing	D&T 2 Tool use	D&T 3 Evaluating	D&T 4 Materials	D&T 5 Breadth
1a	2a	3a	4a	5a
1b	2b	3b	4b	5b
1c	2c			5c
1d	2d			
1e	2e			

PSHE

PSHE1 Confidence and respect	PSHE2 Citizenship	PSHE3 Health	PSHE4 Relationships
1a	2a	3a	4a
1b	2b	3b	4b
1c	2c	3c	4c
1d	2d	3d	4d
1e	2e	3e	4e
	2f	3f	
	2g	3g	
	2h		

ICT

ICT 1 Finding out		ICT2 Ideas	ICT3 Reviewing	ICT4 Breadth
1.1a	1.2a	2a	3a	4a
1.1b	1.2b	2b	3b	4b
1.1c	1.2c	2c	3c	4c
	1.2d			

PE

PE 1 Develop skills	PE 2 Apply skills	PE 3 Evaluate	PE 4 Fitness	PE 5 Breadth
1a	2a	3a	4a	5a dance
1b	2b	3b	4b	5b games
	2c	3c		5c gym

Critical skills	Thinking skills
problem solving	observing
decision making	classifying
critical thinking	prediction
creative thinking	making inferences
communication	problem solving
organisation	drawing conclusions
management	
leadership	

Droppers, syringes and pipettes

Previous experience

Children will have had experience of using droppers and pipettes in the Foundation Stage. They are familiar tools for:

- free play in water trays and boxes indoors and in the garden
- filling and emptying small containers and bottles
- dripping and dropping in creative activities with paint, dye and food colouring
- collecting small amounts of water in corners and the bottom of containers
- mixing and exploring coloured water and other liquids.

The responsive adult

In the early stages of working with these materials it is crucial to continue to observe the children. Only by doing this can you set developmentally appropriate challenges and provocations. The ideas listed here are offered as suggestions; the most exciting challenges will arise from children's own interests and motivations, which will only become apparent as you spend time with them, watching and joining them in their play. As you do this, you will be moving between the three interconnecting roles of observer, co-player, extender described below, and will be able to decide what you need to do next to take the learning forward. In three interconnecting roles, the responsive adult will be:

Observer

- observing
- listening
- interpreting

Co-player

- modelling
- playing alongside
- offering suggestions
- responding sensitively
- initiating with care!

Extender

- discussing ideas
- sharing thinking
- modelling new skills
- asking open questions
- being an informed extender
- instigating ideas and thoughts
- supporting children as they make links in learning
- making possibilities evident
- introducing new ideas and resources
- offering challenges and provocations

Offering challenges and provocations

As children get older they can manage much smaller versions of the tools they have been using in the Foundation Stage. Plastic pipettes, tubing and syringes are very cheap from science supply catalogues on websites.

- Use pipettes and some different colours of food colouring to colour containers of water. How many different shades and colours can you make? What happens if you mix the colours? Can you make shades of the colours by using different amounts of colouring?

- How does a pipette work? Look carefully and talk with a friend about this, and draw a diagram to show how they work. Do syringes work in the same way?

- Find some paper towels and use pipettes to explore how absorbent the towels are.

- Collect some very small containers and bottles. Look around at home and at school to see what you can find. Fill them with water — you may have to use a tiny funnel. Now use pipettes and syringes to get the water out of the containers.

- Colour some water in different shades, and use pipettes and syringes to make patterns on paper, paper towels or tissues.

- Try writing your name or a word on a tissue, using a pipette. Is it easy?

- Paint a piece of strong paper or thin card with clear water. Now use the pipettes and runny paint or coloured water to make pictures on the paper. What happens?

- Fill a container with water. Now use a pipette to completely empty the container without touching the water or the container.

- Find some plastic sheeting or a piece cut from a plastic carrier bag. Use the pipettes and syringes to explore how water behaves when you drop it on plastic.

Ready for more?

♦ Fill a tall transparent container with clear water. Use droppers and pipettes to drop inks or undiluted food colouring into the water. Do it a drop at a time and watch what happens. Take some photos. Try adding another colour. What happens now?

♦ Work with friend to find a way to catch a drop of colouring underwater after it has been dropped. How easy is this to do?

♦ Use colourings to make a range of shades of one colour. Find a way to record the range of shades you make.

♦ Using just red, blue and yellow colourings, can you make these colours? Green, brown, pink, orange, purple, black and grey.

♦ Why do you think doctors use syringes to give injections to people and animals? See if you can find out from books and the internet.

♦ Use a syringe with a measure on the side to measure exact amounts of water. Why is it important to be able to measure the amount in the syringe? Why do doctors, dentists, vets, chefs, nurses and animal hunters need to measure carefully when they fill a syringe?

♦ Find some small transparent containers and fill them with sand. Now use pipettes and syringes to explore what happens when you drop or inject water into the sand. Take some photos.

Materials, websites, books and other references

Materials

For syringes, pipettes and tubing suitable for school use:

www.philipharris.co.uk

ASCO Educational www.ascoeducational.co.uk; suppliers of equipment and tools for water play:

Other education suppliers will have more equipment, try;

Eduzone: www.eduzone.co.uk

TTS Group have a wide range of water tools and containers: www.tts-group.co.uk

Get plastic tubing from aquarium suppliers, garden centres and DIY shops.

Food colouring in big bottles from www.tts-group.co.uk

Websites

Fact sheets on water are available on www.bbc.co.uk/health or ga.water.usgs.gov — the US government education site for water with pictures and facts.

Look at www.liquidsculpture.com for some breathtaking images of water drops.

Books

Sand and Water Play: Simple, Creative Activities for Young Children; Sherrie West; Gryphon House

The Little Book of Sand and Water; Sally Featherstone; Featherstone Education

Google images

For images of water try:

• drop
• waterfall
• funnel
• dropper
• pipette.

Guttering and drainpipes

Previous experience

Guttering and drainpipes are now a feature of most early years settings, and the majority of children will have experimented with and explored these resources:

- in free play indoors and out of doors
- in sand and water play
- in focused work on weather and rainfall
- in recreating stories and rhymes such as Incey Wincey Spider
- in imaginative play where pipes and guttering may have been used to represent a variety of objects in scenes, shelters and structures
- in experimentation, making slopes, tunnels, roadways, for moving balls, cars, sand, gravel, rice, water etc.

The responsive adult

In the early stages of working with these materials it is crucial to continue to observe the children. Only by doing this can you set developmentally appropriate challenges and provocations. The ideas listed here are offered as suggestions; the most exciting challenges will arise from children's own interests and motivations, which will only become apparent as you spend time with them, watching and joining them in their play. As you do this, you will be moving between the three interconnecting roles of observer, co-player, extender described below, and will be able to decide what you need to do next to take the learning forward. In three interconnecting roles, the responsive adult will be:

Observer
- observing
- listening
- interpreting

Co-player
- modelling
- playing alongside
- offering suggestions
- responding sensitively
- initiating with care!

Extender
- discussing ideas
- sharing thinking
- modelling new skills
- asking open questions
- being an informed extender
- instigating ideas and thoughts
- supporting children as they make links in learning
- making possibilities evident
- introducing new ideas and resources
- offering challenges and provocations

Offering challenges and provocations

- Can you find ways to join the pipes together so they don't leak? What works best? Try:
  - duct tape
  - gaffer tape
  - sellotape
  - brown parcel tape
  - masking tape

  Can you make a chart or graph to show the results of your experiments?

- Can you make a waterway for small boats?

- Make a waterway with guttering and then use stones, pebbles, sticks, twigs and sand to make a dam.

- Can you build a waterway with two, three, four or five bends or corners?

- Can you invent a way of collecting rainwater using your pipes and guttering? Collect water in different places and measure how much you collect in each place. Which place is best?

- Make a waterfall with guttering — how high can you make it? What can you use to collect the water at the bottom of the waterfall?

- Have a regatta or boat race, using your guttering as a river. Work with your friends to set up the course, choose a small boat each and see how you can make your boat win a race.

- Can you make some boats with sails, and sail them on the river you have made? You could use polystyrene trays, plastic plates or other recycled materials. What is the best way to make the boats move along the guttering and through the pipes?

- Try pouring coloured water down guttering into a bowl of clear water. Watch carefully what happens.

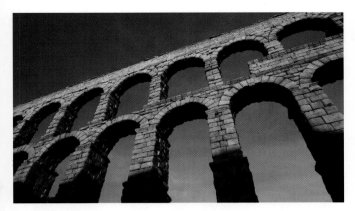

Ready for more?

♦ Use the guttering to make rivers in a small world landscape. Add grass, paths, trees and other objects on the banks of the rivers and streams.

♦ Find out how to play 'Pooh Sticks'. Make a game for yourselves, where you can race small sticks or leaves along a guttering racetrack. How can you make them go faster or slow down?

♦ Google 'waterfalls' and 'white water'. Can you add stones and boulders to your waterway to make white water and rapids?

♦ Use piping in sand to make an underground river or tunnel.

♦ Use the internet and books to research different sorts of water features. Can you create a water feature with the guttering and pipes?

♦ Find a clipboard and go round your school to locate all the guttering and piping you can find. Watch these when it rains and see how they work and if any of them are blocked. Could you invent a tool to unblock drainpipes or guttering?

♦ Find some empty plastic water bottles, make holes in them, and fix them to plastic tubing to make showers or sprinklers.

♦ What is the longest waterway you can make? Can you make a waterway on several levels? Look on the internet for photos of canals and aqueducts.

Materials

Suppliers of plastic piping and other rainwater supplies: Most DIY stores have guttering, drainpipes and other plumbing supplies (builders' merchants may have lower prices) and you could ask parents for contacts in the building trade. Ask parents, colleagues and friends for: old *clean* guttering and drainpipes, hose from washing machines, tumble driers and vacuum cleaners, builders' trays (or cement mixing trays) are very useful for containing the water during experiments. Get these from DIY superstores such as B&Q, Wilkinson's or Homebase. TTS Group **www.tts-group.co.uk** or **www.philipharris.co.uk** have a wide range of equipment.

Get cat litter trays or washing up bowls from a Bargain Shop for space saving water play.

www.plumbworld.co.uk has an incredible variety of branded water pipes, at Internet-only prices,

and **www.screwfix.com** has a vast range of plumbing equipment to look at.

Websites

www.wateraid.org/uk is a site for charity collections to support water aid.

www.kidzone.ws/water has fun facts for kids about the Water Cycle. Including photos, activity suggestions and some printable worksheets.

Google images

For useful images of water and the water cycle, weather and natural features of rain, enter the name of what you want to see:

* plumber
* water cycle
* drain
* aqueduct
* monsoon

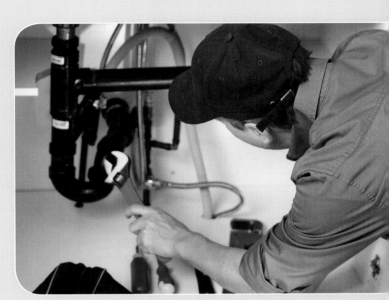

Books

Some suitable books for younger readers include:

Robbie the Raindrop's First Adventure; Rebecca Williams, Author House

The Biography of Splash the Raindrop; Gary Piper; Publish America

The Little Raindrop; Wendy Garrison; Findhorn Press

The Adventures of Robbie the Raindrop; John Carroll; Tate Publishing

The Great Kapok Tree; Lynne Cherry; Harcourt

The Marriage of the Rain Goddess; Margaret Wolfson; Barefoot Books

Rain Tonight: (a Hurricane story); Steve Pitt; Tundra Books

Lila and the Secret of Rain (Kenyan story); David Conway; Frances Lincoln Children's Books

What Makes It Rain? Susan Mayes; Usborne Starting Points

Syphoning

Previous experience

By the time children leave the Foundation Stage they should have had some experience of using simple syphons in water play:

- in free play indoors and out of doors
- in role-play situations
- in play with guttering and drainpipes
- to explore ways of moving water from one level to another
- when playing with buckets, tubing and other simple science equipment.

They should also have had experience of:

- talking about how water moves, and how gravity affects this movement
- using their skills and creativity to make water do what they want.

The responsive adult

In the early stages of working with these materials it is crucial to continue to observe the children. Only by doing this can you set developmentally appropriate challenges and provocations. The ideas listed here are offered as suggestions; the most exciting challenges will arise from children's own interests and motivations, which will only become apparent as you spend time with them, watching and joining them in their play. As you do this, you will be moving between the three interconnecting roles of observer, co-player, extender described below, and will be able to decide what you need to do next to take the learning forward. In three interconnecting roles, the responsive adult will be:

Observer

- observing
- listening
- interpreting

Co-player

- modelling
- playing alongside
- offering suggestions
- responding sensitively
- initiating with care!

Extender

- discussing ideas
- sharing thinking
- modelling new skills
- asking open questions
- being an informed extender
- instigating ideas and thoughts
- supporting children as they make links in learning
- making possibilities evident
- introducing new ideas and resources
- offering challenges and provocations

Offering challenges and provocations

Children may need practice in accepting and carrying out challenges presented by adults, when they have been used to free play in water. You may need to introduce this gradually and sit with the children as they work to encourage them to stay on task!

- Using syphons, funnels and tubes, can you make water travel from one container to another?

- Put a bucket of water on a table, and another bucket on the floor. How can you get the water from the top bucket into the bottom bucket without moving either of the buckets?

- Can you use syphons and other water equipment to make a water feature in your playground? Draw some pictures before you start and take some photos of your finished work.

- Can you use syphons for other substances? Try them with sand, paint, flour, paste. Does a syphon work with all of these? Do you know why?

- Join a syphon to the end of a piece of tubing. Experiment with moving water along the tubing using the syphon. Try with the tubing flat, sloping down and sloping up.

- Can you fix up a series of syphons to move water between two or more containers such as plastic buckets.

- Collect or make some cylinders of different materials — card, rigid plastic, flexible plastic, bubble wrap. Can you use these to make syphons?

- Collect some empty pumps from hand soap or lotions. Use these to find out how hand pumps work. Are they the same as syphons?

Ready for more?

◆ Use the internet to find out how pumps are used in industry. Put 'hand pump' in Google Images and look for some pictures. Then click on some of the pictures and find out more about the websites behind the pictures.

◆ Look up 'fire engine pump' on Google Images.

◆ Then try **people.howstuffworks.com** and search for 'fire engine pump' to find some information and pictures of how fire engines work. You could also look at 'pump' on the same site for information on how washing machine pumps work.

◆ Find some empty hand pumps from soap or hand cream. Use these to make a machine that pumps water from one place to another. You could add plastic tubing and other containers. If you colour the water, it will be easier to see where it's going.

◆ Get a hand-held water spray (the sort for spraying indoor plants). Find out how it works, then think of six different ways to use the spray. It would be better to do this outside! At least one of the uses of the spray must be artistic.

◆ Search the internet, magazines, your school and home to see how many pumps, syphons and sprayers you can find. Don't forget to look under the sink!

Materials, websites, books and other references

Materials

Syphons, plastic tubing and other useful containers from **www.philipharris.co.uk, www.tts-group.co.uk** or educational suppliers.

ASCO **www.ascoeducational.co.uk** have a water play activity workshop and some great aqueduct sets for building big water constructions out of doors.

Get plastic pipettes cheap from **www.esupply.co.uk** - in packs of 100.

There is a huge variety and range of types in suppliers catalogues and on their websites. Many suppliers have 'own brand' versions of water equipment, which are often cheaper, but may not be as durable. As with all educational equipment, you will get what you pay for — buy the best you can afford. For simple water containers such as buckets, bowls, plastic boxes etc. you can go to bargain shops or DIY stores.

Pumps from hand soap and other cosmetics are another free resource, and you could try (clean) plant spray pumps, bike pumps and balloon pumps to explore the principles of syphons and pumping. Fire Stations and Fire Service sites will have information on fire engine pumps.

Websites

Look on **www-saps.plantsci.cam.ac** for information on self watering plants and worksheets lined to the KS1 curriculum, and at **www.woodlands-junior.kent.sch.uk** a school site with activities and worksheets.

www.primaryschoolscience.com/clipart has good clipart of science equipment such as beakers for displays etc - look in the chemistry section.

Some sites with pumping and hose equipment - **www.flexiblehose.co.uk, www.holmeshose.co.uk, www.aflex-hose.co.uk, www.hoseint.co.uk** (drilling platforms).

Books

Starting Point Science; Susan Mayes; Usborne

How it Works; Neil Ardley; Readers Digest

Fire Engines; (Machines and Work); DK

Tonka; If I Could Drive a Fire Truck; Michael Teitelbaum; Cartwheel Books

Oil and Gas; John Zronik; Crabtree

From Oil to Gas; Shannon Zemlicka; Lerner

Oil and Gas; Neil Morris; Smart Apple Media

Rain Gardens; Nigel Dunnett; Timber Press

Water wheels

Previous experience

During their time in the Foundation Stage, children will have played in water trays with pipes, pumps, water wheels and pipettes:

- in free play indoors and out of doors.

They will have used these materials in exploratory and imaginative play and will have begun to explore their potential for moving water from one place to another.

- filling and emptying containers
- spraying and squirting
- lifting water with the wheels
- using the wheels with bubbly and coloured water.

The responsive adult

In the early stages of working with these materials it is crucial to continue to observe the children. Only by doing this can you set developmentally appropriate challenges and provocations. The ideas listed here are offered as suggestions; the most exciting challenges will arise from children's own interests and motivations, which will only become apparent as you spend time with them, watching and joining them in their play. As you do this, you will be moving between the three interconnecting roles of observer, co-player, extender described below, and will be able to decide what you need to do next to take the learning forward. In three interconnecting roles, the responsive adult will be:

Observer

- observing
- listening
- interpreting

Co-player

- modelling
- playing alongside
- offering suggestions
- responding sensitively
- initiating with care!

Extender

- discussing ideas
- sharing thinking
- modelling new skills
- asking open questions
- being an informed extender
- instigating ideas and thoughts
- supporting children as they make links in learning
- making possibilities evident
- introducing new ideas and resources
- offering challenges and provocations

Offering challenges and provocations

The challenge for KS1 teachers lies in providing activities that allow children to draw on this previous experience and extend their knowledge in new and exciting ways.

- Measure a litre of water and then pour it through a water wheel into another container. Can you do this without losing any water? Measure the water at the end and see how much has been lost. Can you find out the difference?

- How many ways can you find of moving water from one container to another? Try these:
  - syphoning
  - using a ladle or a spoon
  - with a pipette
  - making holes in the bottom of a container
  - using a funnel and tubing

  Which one works best? Which is quickest? Which wastes least water?

- Can you construct a water-run using:
  - one water wheel
  - two water wheels
  - three water wheels

  Measure the run - what is the longest you can make?

- Use the internet to find out how water wheels were made and how they worked. Do we still use water wheels now? Where?

- Google 'cascade'. Can you use construction pieces and other materials to make a water cascade. Photograph it.

- Can you use ropes and pulleys to lift water out of doors? Try using a climbing frame or fence to carry the weight.

- Fill a small bucket with water and move it three metres without losing any water. How did you do it? How did you check that you didn't lose any water?

Ready for more?

- Make a collection of washing up liquid bottles. Now find a way of testing them to see which one will squirt water furthest. Can you use the force from the bottles to move objects along the ground?

- Can you use some plastic cups to make a cascade? Find ways of fixing them so they work. Take some photos of your inventions.

- Fill a collection of plant misters or plant sprays with different coloured water. Use these to make patterns and designs on different sorts of surfaces. Which surface works best?

- Make a landscape in a shallow tray, using sand, earth or clay. Can you move water round this landscape

- Try making your own water wheels from plastic, card, old wheels from pushchairs or trikes. You will need to find a way to fix the wheel in a vertical position, so it will turn round, then you can fix water containers onto the wheel.

- Can you make a water play world for Lego or Playmobil people? You could make a water chute, log flume, water slide or helter skelter.

- Add some guttering and drainpipes to your water wheels and make water move further and further. Float objects down the moving water.

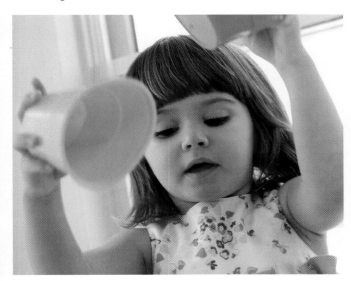

Materials, websites, books and other references

Materials

Making water move has a constant fascination for all humans. Children will use water wheels, guttering and drainpipes to do this, and you may want to add some specialist equipment to make it even more fun:

TTS www.tts-group.co.uk and ASCO www.ascoeducational.co.uk have water viaduct sets as well as water wheels and other simple water equipment.

Google images

For inspiration type in:

- water wheel
- water sculpture
- fountain
- waterfall
- water park
- water chute
- water feature

Websites

www.waterwheelfactory.com or www.leahy-hill.com will take you to working water mills and a water wheel factory. www.reuk.co.uk has an explanation of how water wheels work (click through to 'hydro').

www.williampye.com is a great site for water sculpture — look at 'sources of information' and the 'large and small works' sections and see Brimming Bowl, Scylla and Archimedes.

Books

Pools; Kelly Kline: Rizzoli (architectural coffee table book)

The Water Gardener; John Brookes; Frances Lincoln

Ponds and Lakes; Spotter's Guide; Usborne

Hamish McHaggis: The Wonderful Water Wheel (Hamish Mchaggis) by Linda Strachan and Sally J. Collins; GW Publishing

The Fish and the Water Wheel; Christopher Pilkington; Patmos

Roberto and the Magic Fountain; Donna Vann; Lion Hudson

Little Eagle and the Sacred Waterfall; (Native American Tale); Howard Losness; Universe

The Wonder of a Waterfall; Allan Fowler; Children's Press

The Highest Waterfall; Stuart Kallen; Kidhaven Press

Boats and harbours

Previous experience

Small world boats are a favourite part of water play in the Foundation Stage and at home. Most children will have already spent time exploring:

- aspects of floating and sinking

- boats as part of free play indoors and outside

- making boats, leaves and other objects float in puddles and ponds

- seeing, sailing and riding in boats in parks and at the seaside.

The responsive adult

In the early stages of working with these materials it is crucial to continue to observe the children. Only by doing this can you set developmentally appropriate challenges and provocations. The ideas listed here are offered as suggestions; the most exciting challenges will arise from children's own interests and motivations, which will only become apparent as you spend time with them, watching and joining them in their play. As you do this, you will be moving between the three interconnecting roles of observer, co-player, extender described below, and will be able to decide what you need to do next to take the learning forward. In three interconnecting roles, the responsive adult will be:

Observer

- observing
- listening
- interpreting

Co-player

- modelling
- playing alongside
- offering suggestions
- responding sensitively
- initiating with care!

Extender

- discussing ideas
- sharing thinking
- modelling new skills
- asking open questions
- being an informed extender
- instigating ideas and thoughts
- supporting children as they make links in learning
- making possibilities evident
- introducing new ideas and resources
- offering challenges and provocations

Offering challenges and provocations

- Look for some small plastic boats. Test each one to see how much it will carry before it sinks. Try small stones, lego bricks, plastic animals, spoonfuls of sand and play people.

- Try the test again in water with waves. How can you make some waves? What happens to the boats in the miniature storm?

- Create a small world for your boats. You could make a harbour, a fishing village, or an island. Use books and the internet to help you do this. Use Google Images for pictures of 'fishing boat' 'island' 'fishing boat' 'harbour'.

- Google 'coracle' and find out what it is. Try designing and making one.

- Use recycled materials such as plastic bottles and pots, wood, plasticene, foil dishes etc. to make some boats. Test your boats in water. Which materials work best? Photograph some of your best work.

- How can you make your boat waterproof? What could you use? You could try some of these: PVA glue, plastic, cling film, polythene, paint, foil. Which works best?

- Put 'sailing ships' in Google Images. Can you make a boat with sails?

- Put 'narrow boat' or 'canal barge' in Google Images. Can you design and make your own narrow boat? How much weight will it carry?

- Google 'Vikings'. Can you work with some friends to make a Viking ship?

- Make a boating lake or harbour in some big containers such as plastic bowls, plant pots or ice cream tubs. Find out what you need to make by looking in books or on the internet. Get some friends to help you and take your time so the boating lake is the best you can make it.

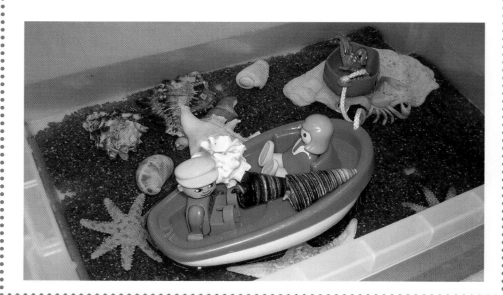

Ready for more?

◆ Can you design a boat that will carry passengers? Start by making a boat that will carry two passengers, then gradually increase your challenge to four, then six, then more.

◆ Choose a soft toy or a bag of small objects such as marbles or Lego bricks. Now design and make a boat that will carry your load.

◆ Make a pirate ship, then make an island for it to sail to. You could make a treasure map and put some characters on your ship. Make a story up with your friends and tell it as you take some photos or video. Invite your friends to a film show of your pirate story.

◆ Use a big piece of board or card and screwed up newspaper to make an island for boats to sail round. Can you put the island in the middle of some water?

◆ Use the Internet to find out all you can about how to make a boat. Now make a PowerPoint presentation or a photo information book with instructions for making a toy boat. Illustrate your book with photos and diagrams.

◆ Get a copy of a story called Treasure Island by Robert Louis Stevenson. Read it yourself or ask someone to read it to you. Make your own book about Treasure Island, with maps, pictures and words.

Materials, websites, books and other references

Materials

Collect all sorts of model boats from bargain toy shops or from educational suppliers. It's also useful to have plenty of plastic containers and other recycled materials for making boats and harbours. Offer different sorts of tape and glues, but make sure there is plenty of waterproof tape (duct tape or similar) to avoid disappointment when they get wet.

Websites

Try some 'big ship' websites such as **www.hms-victory.com** — the official website for HMS Victory, **www.titanic-titanic.com, www.historyonthenet.com** or **www.jorvikviking-centre.co.uk** for Vikings and their ships. Or try **www.cunard.co.uk** and order a cruise brochure.

Google Images

For images of boats and ships, try:

- titanic
- ocean liner
- hms victory

- fishing boat
- power boat
- sailing boat.

Books

Some suitable books for younger readers include:

Inside the Titanic; Ken Marschall; Little,Brown

Ships, Look inside Cross sections: Moir Butterfield; DK

The Story of Ships; Jane Bingham; Usborne

Stephen Biesty's Cross Sections; Stephen Biesty; DK

Titanic; Anna Claybourne; Usborne

Water and Boats; Jon Richards; Franklin Watts

Boats; Ian Rohr; A&C Black

Brilliant Boats; Tony Mitton; Kingfisher Books

The Little Boat; Kathy Henderson; Walker Books

The Goodbye Boat; Mary Joslin; Lion Hudson

All Afloat on Noah's Boat; Tony Mitton; Orchard Books

The Boat; Helen Ward; Simply Read

Ebb and Flo and the New Friend; Jane Simmons; Aladdin

The Green Ship; Quentin Blake; Red Fox

The Sea Monster; Christopher Wormell; Red Fox

Underwater worlds

Previous experience

Playing with small world and fantasy characters is a favourite for most children, and seems to particularly appeal to boys. In the Foundation Stage they will probably have:

- used small world figures in water and sand play
- watched videos and DVDs containing sequences in underwater worlds
- watched and replayed scenes from superhero movies they have seen on TV or video
- listened to stories about underwater worlds
- explored underwater movement and stories in outdoor play, role-play and other creative activities.

The responsive adult

In the early stages of working with these materials it is crucial to continue to observe the children. Only by doing this can you set developmentally appropriate challenges and provocations. The ideas listed here are offered as suggestions; the most exciting challenges will arise from children's own interests and motivations, which will only become apparent as you spend time with them, watching and joining them in their play. As you do this, you will be moving between the three interconnecting roles of observer, co-player, extender described below, and will be able to decide what you need to do next to take the learning forward. In three interconnecting roles, the responsive adult will be:

Observer

- observing
- listening
- interpreting

Co-player

- modelling
- playing alongside
- offering suggestions
- responding sensitively
- initiating with care!

Extender

- discussing ideas
- sharing thinking
- modelling new skills
- asking open questions
- being an informed extender
- instigating ideas and thoughts
- supporting children as they make links in learning
- making possibilities evident
- introducing new ideas and resources
- offering challenges and provocations

Offering challenges and provocations

In KS1 you could provide small world figures of divers, pirates, mermaids, mermen and other characters such as sea monsters, underwater creatures, plastic bowls and aquariums, aquarium plants and rocks.

- Can you make an underwater adventure world for pirates and divers? Can you...
  - make a story where a pirate ship sinks, the pirates lose their treasure, and it is discovered by divers?
  - photograph your story at various stages to use as a PowerPoint presentation, a photo display or a book?

- Could you make an underwater world for mermaids, mermen and sea monsters. You could make caves with stones and weeds from green or orange plastic carriers cut into leaf shapes. Weight these down by tying the plants to stones. Now make a story about the underwater world.

- Make an information book or poster about underwater worlds. Find some pictures of creatures and habitats by looking on the internet and downloading some photos. Find out about habitats and food.

- Set a challenge for your friend. Bury some treasure in an underwater world and let them find the objects. Give them some clues so they know what to look for.

- Google 'Sea-life Adventure' and find out all you can about sharks and tropical fish.

- Find out all you can about the Loch Ness Monster. Now use some Lego to make a monster of your own and make an underwater habitat for it.

- Make a water world for Nemo or The Little Mermaid, or another underwater film.

- Try a superhero underwater scene with Superman, Spiderman or your own favourite superhero.

Ready for more?

♦ Make some underwater worlds in unusual containers — plastic bottles, bowls, fish tanks or food containers.

♦ Find out everything you can about Atlantis. Now use plastic construction pieces to make your own version of Atlantis or another underwater city. When you have built your city, find a really big waterproof container and flood your city with water. Take some photos or a video of what you did.

♦ Write some messages to put in bottles. You could try all sorts and sizes of bottles, just make sure they are plastic, so they float. You could float your bottles in a water tray, an aquarium or down plastic guttering or drainpipes. You could write letters, jokes, questions, challenges, riddles, puzzles or anything else!

♦ Buy some old crockery from a charity shop. Photograph it, then put it in a strong plastic bag and smash it up. Bury the pieces in an underwater world and see if your friends can use the photos to re-assemble the pieces into the originals.

♦ Find out about shipwrecks, and make shipwreck scenes from recycled materials. Try 'Mary Rose' or 'Titanic' in Google.

♦ Bury plastic letters, numbers, coins or plastic minibeasts in your underwater world for others to discover.

Materials

Educational suppliers have plenty of small world resources that are ideal for underwater scenes and adventures. Try to collect a range of these that can be offered in small containers or baskets to inspire stories and environments:

■ underwater creatures, fish, crabs etc

■ small superhero figures and fantasy underwater figures such as mermaids and pirates

■ underwater monsters and dinosaurs

■ models from films such as Finding Nemo or Shark Tale.

There are also lots of free and cheap resources you could collect with the children:

■ beads, sequins, jewels and foreign coins

■ small boxes and caskets from gifts and other packaging

■ buttons, plastic and metal charms, toys from crackers

■ small items from aquariums — leaves, plants, buildings

■ shells, pebbles and stones, coloured sand and gravel.

Google images

• underwater

• sea bed

• wreck

• **ship in a bottle** will bring up lots of pictures

or

• Atlantis

• mermaid

• treasure

• **Loch Ness Monster** will give help with imagined worlds.

Books

Summer of the Sea Serpent; (Magic Tree House), Mary Pope Osborne

The Sea Monster; Christopher Wormell; Jonathan Cape

Why Can't I Live Underwater Like the Fish? Sally Hewitt; Belitha Press

A Whale of a Tale; Bonnie Worth; Random House (Cat in the Hat)

Mrs Armitage and the Big Wave; Quentin Blake; Red Fox

Pirates Most Wanted; John Matthews; Atheneum Books

Sinbad the Sailor; Gillian Doherty; Usborne

Master Salt the Sailor; Allan Ahlberg; Puffin Books

Pat the Cat and Sailor Sam; Margaret Wilde; Southwood Books

Sailor Mouse; Peter Curry; Picture Lions

Treasure Island; Robert Louis Stevenson; Audio CD

Pirate Pete; Kim Kennedy; Harry Abrahams

Coloured water

Previous experience

Changing the colour of water is something that fascinates young children from the earliest age. During the Foundation Stage they will have explored some of the following:

- coloured and colouring water indoors and outside, with and without tools such as piping, tubes and containers
- mixing paint
- adding food colouring to icing, jelly etc
- changing colours in food, such as making soup, fruit salad, smoothies, juices
- mixing their own drinks at snack time
- playing with coloured water and 'tea' in role-play
- experiments with ice, snow, puddle water and other natural materials.

The responsive adult

In the early stages of working with these materials it is crucial to continue to observe the children. Only by doing this can you set developmentally appropriate challenges and provocations. The ideas listed here are offered as suggestions; the most exciting challenges will arise from children's own interests and motivations, which will only become apparent as you spend time with them, watching and joining them in their play. As you do this, you will be moving between the three interconnecting roles of observer, co-player, extender described below, and will be able to decide what you need to do next to take the learning forward. In three interconnecting roles, the responsive adult will be:

Observer

- observing
- listening
- interpreting

Co-player

- modelling
- playing alongside
- offering suggestions
- responding sensitively
- initiating with care!

Extender

- discussing ideas
- sharing thinking
- modelling new skills
- asking open questions
- being an informed extender
- instigating ideas and thoughts
- supporting children as they make links in learning
- making possibilities evident
- introducing new ideas and resources
- offering challenges and provocations

Offering challenges and provocations

Provide children with all sorts of substances that can colour water — food colouring, paint, fruit and vegetables, tea, coffee, earth, clay etc. Allow plenty of time for free exploration of these substances to see which are most effective. See opposite for some ideas.

- Use the colourings in your classroom to experiment with mixing colours. See how you can make shades of the same colour or new colours. Paint these on paper so you have a record of all the different colours and shades you have made.

- Use some of the colourings you have in your room to make paints. Now make some pictures with the new paints and display them with the colourings you used.

- Use the internet to find out how people made paints, dyes and colourings for fabrics and pictures before they could buy them from shops.

- Use some of this information to make your own dyes and pigments and try them on all sorts of fabrics. get some clothes from a charity shop or rummage sale.

- Use the newly dyed fabrics to make decorative hangings or weavings — you could tie them to an old bike wheel, a hoop or some garden netting.

- Find out how to do tie-dye. Now collect the things you need for tie-dying some of your own creations. Start with smaller pieces of fabric, then you could decorate your own white teeshirt.

- Batik is another way of decorating fabric. You might have a book in your school that shows you how to do it, or you could put 'Batik' into Google and Google Images to find out. Try this method of making patterns on fabric.

- Collect a range of clear plastic containers and fill them with different coloured waters. Put them on a window ledge to make an interesting display.

Ready for more?

- Make a 'giant coloured water' display outside. Use tubes, plastic bottles and containers, and other clear boxes and bowls. Can you make a sculpture with moving water?

- Fill glass bottles with coloured water to make musical bottles. Devise a notation system using the colours and compose some bottle music.

- Make some shades of colours using food colouring. Use these shades to paint pictures or patterns.

- Collect some absorbent papers (blotting paper, sugar paper, kitchen roll). Use droppers to make pictures and designs with coloured water.

- Use food colouring on damp paper and watch how the colours behave. Can you control the way they do it? Draw some coloured lines on tissues or white kitchen roll with felt pens. Drape the pieces over rulers so the edge JUST touches some water in a bowl. Watch what happens! Dry the paper flat and use it for art work.

- Use food colouring, dyes or paint to colour ice. Freeze the ice in ice cube trays or other containers and then photograph the results. Look carefully at what happens to the colouring when the water freezes.

- Get some water-based inks from an art shop and experiment with these. Use them for painting, writing or other marks.

Materials, websites, books and other references

Materials

Batik and tie-dye equipment and simple Batik techniques available from Fred Aldous **www.aldous.co.uk**

Food dyes (also good for dyeing fabrics and paper) in large quantities, and inks from TTS Group **www.tts-group.co.uk**

Some fruit and vegetables give cheap dyes - try blackberries (dark blue), onion skins (yellow), beetroot or red plums (dark red). Coffee and tea make easy dyes.

For information on natural dyes try **www.thenaturaldyestudio.com** or **www.pioneerthinking.com/naturaldyes** which is a USA site, but has lots of information on what to use and how to prepare the dyes.

Google Images

- tie-dye
- natural dyes
- Batik
- natural weaving
- inks

or

- cave painting
- Lascaux

to find out about cave paintings, which were made from mixtures of natural materials

or

- Holi (an Indian festival where everyone gets painted!)

Books

Batik and Tie-Dye; Nancy Belfer; Dover Publications

Fabric to Dye for; Susie Stokoe; Southwater

Tie-Dye Your Teeshirt; Moira Butterfield; Bloomsbury

Berry Smudges and Leaf Prints; Elaine Senisi; Dutton Books

The Art and Craft of Natural Dyeing; J N Liles; University of Tennessee

A Dyer's Garden; Rita Buchanan; Interweave Press

Wild Colour; Jenny Dean; Mitchell Beazley

Quennu and the Cave Bear; Marie Day; Tandem

Caves of Lascaux; Brad Burnham; Powerkids press

Blackberry Ink (poems); Eve Merriman; William Morrow

Colour (How Artists use...); Paul Flux; Heinemann

Using Colour; Isabelle Thomas; Raintree

Light and Colour; Malcolm Dixon; Evans

Elmer The Elephant; David McKee; Andersen Press

Adding things to water

Previous experience

During the early years, children will have experimented widely with adding things to water.

These may have included:

- free play indoors and out of doors
- making dough
- cold and hot cooking activities
- in sand and water play
- working with clay, dough and other malleable materials
- making glue and paste;
- mixing paint
- washing dolls, dolls' clothes, construction toys, vehicles
- mixing their own drinks.

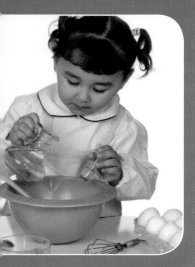

The responsive adult

In the early stages of working with these materials it is crucial to continue to observe the children. Only by doing this can you set developmentally appropriate challenges and provocations. The ideas listed here are offered as suggestions; the most exciting challenges will arise from children's own interests and motivations, which will only become apparent as you spend time with them, watching and joining them in their play. As you do this, you will be moving between the three interconnecting roles of observer, co-player, extender described below, and will be able to decide what you need to do next to take the learning forward. In three interconnecting roles, the responsive adult will be:

Observer

- observing
- listening
- interpreting

Co-player

- modelling
- playing alongside
- offering suggestions
- responding sensitively
- initiating with care!

Extender

- discussing ideas
- sharing thinking
- modelling new skills
- asking open questions
- being an informed extender
- instigating ideas and thoughts
- supporting children as they make links in learning
- making possibilities evident
- introducing new ideas and resources
- offering challenges and provocations

Offering challenges and provocations

Encourage children to add objects and substances to water and watch what happens. They may need encouragement from you, and opportunities to select from a wide range of resources to mix and add to plain or coloured water.

- Can you make your own perfume by adding flower petals, herbs, citrus peel etc to water?

- How is bubble bath made? Can you make your own bubble bath from the ingredients in your classroom?

- Make your own sorbets, ice lollies, fruit juices by adding fruit and flavours to water.

- Try mixing cooking oil into water. What happens? Take photos of the different ways you tried to make the oil and water mix together.

- Make some fruit drinks with whole fruit, fruit juices and water. Carry out a 'tasting test' and record everyone's favourites. Make a graph of your findings.

- Use flour and water to make your own glue. Experiment with different amounts of glue and water. Test the strength of the glue.

- Make some porridge with different amounts of water to make thin and thick mixtures. Ask your friends to choose between the thick or thin porridge.

- Collect some different sorts of foods (tea leaves, coffee, salt, sugar, margarine, flour). Mix some of each food with water. Which ones dissolve? Think about how you could get the food out of the water again.

- Mix some icing sugar and water and use this to decorate some biscuits or bought buns.

- Use a runny mixture of icing sugar and water to paint over the surface of some paper. Now use a dropper top to drop food colouring on the wet paper. Watch what happens. Take some photos.

Ready for more?

♦ Explore making fizzy water. Use bicarbonate of soda, soluble vitamin tablets or Alka Seltzer tablets. How do they work? Why don't they fizz in the packet?

♦ Find out what happens if you add bicarbonate of soda to water? Make an experiment and take a series of photos of what happens — you may have to do the experiment several times to get the photos! Now make your photos into a worksheet to help other people to do your experiment.

♦ Add straw and mud to water and make your own bricks. What could you use for a mould? Do you want big or small bricks? Leave the bricks to dry and then make a structure or model. Google 'build a mud hut' to find out about Cob houses.

♦ Make bubble mixture with water and washing up liquid. Add a few drops of glycerine to make the bubbles stronger. Now make some of your own bubble blowers from soft wire. Experiment till you find the best one. Take photos of the best and biggest bubbles.

♦ Collect a lot of different recycled materials — plastic, card, paper, fabric. Test these to see which ones dissolve in water and how long it takes. Record your findings.

♦ What happens when vegetables are cooked in boiling water? Look at some raw vegetables and some cooked ones to find out.

Materials

You can add anything to water:

■ food substances, such as salt, flour, sugar, icing sugar, cornflour, coffee, tea, vinegar or milk

■ natural substances, such as mud, sand, clay, peat, spices or herbs

■ natural objects, such as leaves, berries, seeds, petals, stalks, bark or grass

■ things that don't mix, such as cooking oils, aromatherapy oils or bath oils

■ household liquids, such as washing up liquid, shampoo or hand soap (check they are safe!)

■ things intended for mixing with water, such as noodles, jelly, squashes, paste or plaster.

Mixing these and adding colouring makes for endless different colours and textures.

Google Images

Try searching **cob cottage** for buildings made from mud or

• natural dyes   • colour mixture

• paste   • cornflour

Books

Some books about mixtures and some about cooking:

Super Science Concoctions: 50 Mysterious Mixtures for Fabulous Fun (Williamson Kids Can! Books) by Jill Frankel Hauser and Michael Kline; Williamson

Mixtures and Compounds; Alistair Smith; EDC Publishing

Mixtures and Solutions; Louise Spilsbury; Heinemann

Kids' Crazy Concoctions; J F Hauser; Williamson

Snacktivities; MaryAnn Kohl; Roundhouse

Kids Can Cook; Dorothy Bates; Book Publishing Co

No Cook Cookery; Ting Morris; Sea to Sea

Cold Drinks; Ann Redmayne; Evans

Smoothies; Ann Acres Johnson; Klutz

Berry Smudges and Leaf Prints; Ellen Senisi; Dutton

Nature's Playground; Fiona Danks; Chicago Review Press

Ice

Previous experience

Most children will have had experience of naturally occurring ice, but even this is a less frequent event with climate change and safety concerns. Some children will have:

- played with ice at home
- experienced watching ice in drinks
- made ice lollies
- played with ice shapes and cubes in water trays
- explored ice in puddles, ditches and ponds.

The responsive adult

In the early stages of working with these materials it is crucial to continue to observe the children. Only by doing this can you set developmentally appropriate challenges and provocations. The ideas listed here are offered as suggestions; the most exciting challenges will arise from children's own interests and motivations, which will only become apparent as you spend time with them, watching and joining them in their play. As you do this, you will be moving between the three interconnecting roles of observer, co-player, extender described below, and will be able to decide what you need to do next to take the learning forward. In three interconnecting roles, the responsive adult will be:

Observer

- observing
- listening
- interpreting

Co-player

- modelling
- playing alongside
- offering suggestions
- responding sensitively
- initiating with care!

Extender

- discussing ideas
- sharing thinking
- modelling new skills
- asking open questions
- being an informed extender
- instigating ideas and thoughts
- supporting children as they make links in learning
- making possibilities evident
- introducing new ideas and resources
- offering challenges and provocations

Offering challenges and provocations

Children will need to explore ice in free play before using it in experiments or adult-directed activities. Try just offering a bag of ice cubes (either bought from a supermarket or made yourself). Tip it into a bowl or onto a builder's tray for free play. Offer gloves if children need them — most won't want them! Warn them not to eat the cubes!

- How high can you build with the ice cubes? Are they easy to build with?

- Can you build an igloo with the ice cubes?

- Find some small world figures (polar bears, penguins, eskimos etc) and make an environment for them with the ice cubes.

- Put one ice cube on a table, one outside the door and one in your hand. Which one melts first? Do you know why this happens? Try the same experiment with a few friends — each holding a cube in their hand.

These challenges need access to a freezer or ice making compartment of a fridge.

- Fill some plastic containers, cups, yogurt pots or margarine tubs with water. Use a dropper to add a few drops of food colouring to each container. Put the containers in the freezer overnight. Tip the ice out and see what has happened. Take some photos.

- Try making ice shapes in unusual containers — a rubber glove, a wellington boot, a beach bucket shaped like a castle or a plastic bag tied at the top. Use coloured water if you like.

- Fill a bowl with cold water and tip some ice cubes or ice shapes into the water. What happens to the ice cubes? Take just six photos to show what happens over time. You will need to think about when you take them! Make a display of your findings.

- Make some ice lollies with fruit juice and water.

Ready for more?

♦ Find an ice cube tray. Put small things in each of the sections — beads, sequins, little pictures, buttons or coins. Fill the tray with water or coloured water and freeze it. Tip the cubes out when they have frozen. Now look up 'ice cube scramble' in Google Images and click through to information about an Ice Cube Scramble in America where children scramble for ice cubes with toys and tokens inside.

♦ Go outside and collect some leaves, twigs, petals, small flowers and seeds. Now find some shallow containers — lids, plastic trays and polystyrene trays. Make patterns with your natural objects and very gently fill the containers with water. Add a piece of string or ribbon to the edge (so you can hang it up) and freeze your pattern. When it is frozen, take it out of the container and hang it up out of doors.

♦ Try the same method with bird food and other seeds and hang it up in winter for the birds to peck at.

♦ Look up 'ice sculpture' in Google Images and see what you can find. Some of the images on this page come from **www.icechef.com** — see what else he has made. The goldfish are real and they are swimming in real water!

♦ Try making a frozen fish tank with some plastic fish and weeds made from green plastic strips in green water, then freeze it.

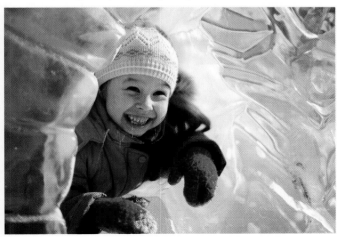

Materials, websites, books and other references

Materials

Access to a freezer or fridge is fairly essential, but you could make ice shapes at home, or encourage the children to do so. If you need to transport them, use a freezer bag, or ice packs, or just wrap the ice in a thick layer of newspaper or a blanket and put it in a plastic bag. It should stay frozen for at least an hour. If the children experiment with unusual ice moulds, they could leave the ice in these and bring them to school before they tip it out. Most supermarkets sell ice cubes in bags. They cost under a pound for a big bag, and they are suitable for all sorts of experiments.

Get ice packs from **www.lakeland.co.uk** or your local supermarket, and try Pound Shops for unusual ice cube trays and drink coolers (shapes to freeze to drop into drinks, like the penguins on the left).

Google Images

- icicle
- icicle lights
- ice cube moulds

and some inspiration may come by trying

- ice sculpture
- igloo
- ice cave
- glacier
- iceberg.

Websites

Look at www.icechef.com for some wonderful examples of ice carving and photos of the ice chef at work, or Google **Ice Festivals** for some great pictures from the BBC of the Japanese Ice Festival.

Or www.blackjackbuffers.com for photos of Russian ice sculptures or www.thisisthelife.com for Ice sculptures in Alaska.

Also try www.iceicleinn.com where there is an ice cube scramble for kids that might be worth replicating in school! Andy Goldsworthy, the sculptor has had some fun with big snowballs - try Andy Goldsworthy snowballs in Google.

Books

Matsumara's Ice Sculpture: Prokos; Longman

Ice and Snow Drawings; Andy Goldsworthy; Fruitmarket Gallery

Winter Nature Activities for Children; Dagmar Israel; Floris Books

Nature's Playground; Fiona Danks; Frances Lincoln

Building and Igloo; Ulli Steltzer; Henry Holt

Measuring water

Previous experience

Jugs, measuring beakers and cups are familiar equipment in the Foundation Stage, and most children will have done some experimenting:

- in free play indoors and outside;
- with filling and emptying;
- in stacking and nesting different sizes of containers;
- in scooping, pouring, ladling and tipping liquids and solids such as sand.

The responsive adult

In the early stages of working with these materials it is crucial to continue to observe the children. Only by doing this can you set developmentally appropriate challenges and provocations. The ideas listed here are offered as suggestions; the most exciting challenges will arise from children's own interests and motivations, which will only become apparent as you spend time with them, watching and joining them in their play. As you do this, you will be moving between the three interconnecting roles of observer, co-player, extender described below, and will be able to decide what you need to do next to take the learning forward. In three interconnecting roles, the responsive adult will be:

Observer

- observing
- listening
- interpreting

Co-player

- modelling
- playing alongside
- offering suggestions
- responding sensitively
- initiating with care!

Extender

- discussing ideas
- sharing thinking
- modelling new skills
- asking open questions
- being an informed extender
- instigating ideas and thoughts
- supporting children as they make links in learning
- making possibilities evident
- introducing new ideas and resources
- offering challenges and provocations

Offering challenges and provocations

- Find some recycled containers of different sizes (yogurt pots, milk, water or juice bottles etc). Now estimate which one holds most, which holds least. Put them in the order you decided on, and take a photo. Now use water to find out the capacity of each container. After your experiment, put the containers in the order of their capacity and take another photo. Were you right?

- Get some spoons of different sizes and three containers of different sizes. Can you use these to find out how many spoonfuls each container holds. Use your brain and plan well. You may find a clever way to do it!

- Get an egg cup, a plastic cup and a bucket. Use these to find out how many egg cups of water fill the bucket. Work with a friend to think and plan before you start.

- Find some recycled containers with printing on them. Look for the place where the amount of the contents is written. It will say something like 4fl oz (120ml). Put the containers in order of their capacity. Is this the same as the order of their size?

- Now use these containers to check for accuracy. For this investigation you need some plastic beakers with measurements marked on them. Use these to check the capacity of the containers you found, to see if the labelling is accurate. What do you find? Why could this be?

- Find a plastic water bottle. Can you make your own measuring beaker from this, using a permanent marker? Take some photos of all the different stages of making your measuring beaker.

Ready for more?

◆ Use the internet or a book to find out about litres, centilitres and millilitres. Now use the methods you found for making beakers from recycled materials to make measuring beakers of different sizes. Try to find different sized containers for the different capacities, and mark them with a permanent marker.

◆ Fill some plastic beakers with water to the top measurement level. Now try dropping objects gently into the beakers. What happens to the water level? Why might this be? Does the same thing happen with every object you put in? Try using pebbles, Lego bricks, conkers or coins. What happens if you use ice cubes?

◆ Now use what you found out to calculate how much space the following things take in water:

- 6 Lego bricks
- 14 pebbles
- an empty water bottle
- a full water bottle
- 4 play people.

Record what you find out.

◆ Do the same investigation with a house brick. Put water in a bowl and measure the surface level. Put the brick in carefully and measure the level again. Wait ten minutes and measure again. What has happened? Why do you think that is?

Materials

Try to collect as many different sorts of containers and measuring vessels as you can. They could be:

■ Recycled containers such as yoghurt pots, plastic spoons, water bottles, juice bottles, plastic containers from milk, washing up liquid or detergents

■ Kitchen equipment (try bargain shops, charity shops and markets) such as plastic jugs, measuring spoons and scoops

■ Science equipment such as measuring beakers, measuring spoons, pipettes, plastic test tubes and funnels

■ Don't forget to add some very small containers, such as those from perfumes, aromatherapy oils and spices.

If you can afford to buy something from an educational supplier, try **www.new.craftpacks.co.uk** for measuring beakers, or ask your science co-ordinator for their suppliers. Many educational suppliers' catalogues have water measuring equipment, sometimes the Early Years section is best for finding equipment for KS1 children to use independently. Add some tubing and funnels. Get very small funnels from aromatherapy oil suppliers.

Websites

www.metric.org.uk/whatis/definitions has useful conversion charts for liquids and solids such as: 1 litre = 10 décilitres = 100 centilitres = 1000 millilitres.

Materials, websites, books and other references

Google Images

- measuring containers
- measuring jugs
- funnel
- measuring spoons.

Books

Capacity; Henry Pluckrose; Franklin Watts

Measuring; Ruth Merttens; Scholastic

Measuring: Key Stage 1; Barbara Raper; Scholastic

Rain and Snow, measuring the weather; Heinemann

Starting Off with Measuring; Peter Patilla; OUP

Measuring (start Maths); Ann Montague-Smith; QED

Divers and diving

Previous experience

In the Foundation Stage, children may have had experience of using toy divers in water play, in role-play, or they may have experimented with underwater swimming. These experiences might have included:

- in small world play
- in experiments and observations
- in full role-play with flippers and goggles
- on holiday in swimming pools and the sea
- watching underwater films on DVD or film
- experimenting with submerging things such as water bottles in water play

The responsive adult

In the early stages of working with these materials it is crucial to continue to observe the children. Only by doing this can you set developmentally appropriate challenges and provocations. The ideas listed here are offered as suggestions; the most exciting challenges will arise from children's own interests and motivations, which will only become apparent as you spend time with them, watching and joining them in their play. As you do this, you will be moving between the three interconnecting roles of observer, co-player, extender described below, and will be able to decide what you need to do next to take the learning forward. In three interconnecting roles, the responsive adult will be:

Observer

- observing
- listening
- interpreting

Co-player

- modelling
- playing alongside
- offering suggestions
- responding sensitively
- initiating with care!

Extender

- discussing ideas
- sharing thinking
- modelling new skills
- asking open questions
- being an informed extender
- instigating ideas and thoughts
- supporting children as they make links in learning
- making possibilities evident
- introducing new ideas and resources
- offering challenges and provocations

Offering challenges and provocations

- Use water bottles to experiment with making submarines. How can you make them sink? Can you make them come up again?

- Why do humans need face masks and snorkels? Find out from the internet or books.

- Can you make a mask and snorkel from recycled materials? Why won't this work in a real swimming pool?

- Find some plastic tubing and experiment with blowing bubbles like a diver. What happens if you suck? Why does the end of a diver's snorkel stick up out of the water?

- Find out how long you can hold your breath for. Sit down while you do this test, because it may make you feel dizzy! Who can hold their breath for the longest? Use a stopwatch to find out.

- Look up water diving beetles on the internet. Make a fact sheet of the things you find out. Get someone to help you to download some photos or drawings.

- Find some small world people or superheroes. Can you make a diving bell or submarine for them to travel in?

- Make a marine habitat for your submarine in an aquarium or water tray, using rocks, shells, plastic aquarium plants and other objects.

- Float a sponge on the surface of some water. Can you make the sponge sink? How did you do it?

- Tie a small world person or a superhero figure onto a piece of string. Now dip it in a bowl or bucket of water. What happens? How can you make the figure sink to the bottom of the water? and how can you make it come up again? Think carefully about what you can use to weight the figure. Try several different ways. Which works best?

- Find out about the Great Diving Beetle **www.arkive.org**. How does this beetle breathe underwater?

Ready for more?

◆ Some insects and animals can hold their breath for a long time — look in books and on the internet to find out about beavers, otters, whales, turtles, hippos and others. How many different animals can you find that usually live on land, but can swim underwater?

◆ Can you find out how a real submarine works? Do a labelled drawing of this so you can explain it to someone else.

◆ How do flippers work? Look at some pictures of divers and of big fish. Can you see how the flippers work to make the diver swim faster?

◆ Look on the internet at: **www.kids-science-experiments.com** Find the floating and sinking experiments and find out how to make a toy diver from a pen top and some Plasticine. Make several of these divers with your friends and see which one is best.

◆ Try some more experiments from this site and from other sites you find when you Google 'science experiments kids'.

◆ See if you can find a cheap diving toy in a toy shop. Does it work in the same way as the diver you made?

◆ Go to **www.psbkids.org** and find the experiment called Dancing Raisins. Collect the things you need (from home or school) and try this experiment with a friend. What makes the raisins dance?

Materials

www.amazon.co.uk supply all the toy submarines shown in this book. You can also get divers from toy catalogues and websites selling toys.

Collect bottles and small plastic containers for experiments, and offer plastic fish tanks or washing up bowls for trials.

The diving photos on these pages can be found on **www.aquaturtle.co.uk**, a diving school for kids.

Google Images

- diver
- submarine
- underwater
- river bed
- scuba diving
- tropical fish
- sub-aqua
- Jacques Cousteau

Websites

Try **www.kids-science-experiments.com** for experiments in floating and sinking, or Google simple science experiments for kids and how to make divers from simple objects.

Materials, websites, books and other references

Books

What's under the Sea?; Sophie Tahta; Usborne

Snail and the Whale; Julia Donaldson; Macmillan

Dougal's Deep-sea Diary (Paperback); by Simon Bartram; Templar

Lemmy Was a Diver; Colin McNaughton; Andersen

The Pearl Diver; Julia Johnson; Stacey International

Why Can't I Live Underwater with the Fish; Sally Hewitt; Belitha Press

Four Corners, Underwater Treasures; Maureen Haselhurst; Longman

Underwater World; Angela Wilkes; Two-Can

One Night in the Coral Sea; B Sneer; Charlesbridge Publishing

Inside a Coral Reef; Carole Telford; Heinemann

Coral Reef; Caroline Bingham; DK

This is the Reef; Miriam Moss; Frances Lincoln

Over in the Ocean; In a Coral Reef; Marianne Berks; Dawn Publications

Submarine; Neil Mallard; DK

Commotion in the Ocean; Giles Andreae; Orchard Books

Jelly and other additions

Previous experience

Throughout their time in the Foundation Stage, children will have been involved in jelly making. They may have:

- helped to make jelly for parties or to eat at snack time
- played with jelly in the sand and water trays
- explored the properties of jelly in early science and language activities
- explored the language and vocabulary of describing jelly and how it looks, behaves and feels
- used jelly to make landscapes and environments for small world play
- mixed objects and small toys with jelly and watched them set
- used moulds to make jelly shapes.

The responsive adult

In the early stages of working with these materials it is crucial to continue to observe the children. Only by doing this can you set developmentally appropriate challenges and provocations. The ideas listed here are offered as suggestions; the most exciting challenges will arise from children's own interests and motivations, which will only become apparent as you spend time with them, watching and joining them in their play. As you do this, you will be moving between the three interconnecting roles of observer, co-player, extender described below, and will be able to decide what you need to do next to take the learning forward. In three interconnecting roles, the responsive adult will be:

Observer

- observing
- listening
- interpreting

Co-player

- modelling
- playing alongside
- offering suggestions
- responding sensitively
- initiating with care!

Extender

- discussing ideas
- sharing thinking
- modelling new skills
- asking open questions
- being an informed extender
- instigating ideas and thoughts
- supporting children as they make links in learning
- making possibilities evident
- introducing new ideas and resources
- offering challenges and provocations

Offering challenges and provocations

Some of these provocations will need preparation, but once children get used to the properties of jelly, they can do the preparation as part of the activity, or prepare things for others.

- Make a jelly with small fruit or objects in it. Now get your friends to guess and write down how many raspberries, blueberries, fish, marbles are set in your jelly. Now find out and count them to check (you will have to take them out of the jelly!). Who was right? Who was nearest? Set up a new challenge with some more jelly and objects. Make sure you can see the objects by using transparent containers.

- Use jelly to create:
  - a lunar landscape
  - a swamp
  - a dinosaur world
  - a fairy forest

  Add small world figures, leaves and twigs, stones and pebbles to your world. Now make up a story and take photos of each scene. Make a book or a PowerPoint presentation for your friends to look at.

- Make some different shaped small jellies in pots or moulds. Use these to make a sculpture. Make sure you take some photos to preserve your work of art!

- Can you make a striped jelly with more than one colour? How can you do this?

- When you know how to make a striped jelly, make one where the stripes are:
  - uneven widths or
  - sloping or
  - vertical.

  Record how you did it, so your friends can do it too. Make a display or book of your instructions and photos with your jellies.

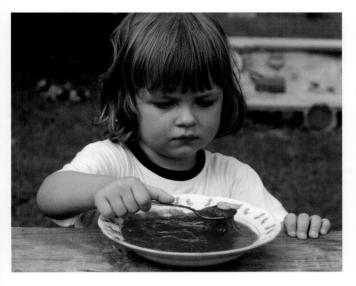

Ready for more?

♦ Bury items in chopped up jelly and set up a treasure hunt for your friends. Make a chart showing all the objects and see how long it takes to find them all. Have some VERY tiny objects to make the challenge even more difficult, but make sure they aren't things that dissolve!

♦ Make lots of small jellies in yogurt pots or the supermarket plastic trays that yoghurts come in. Now see if you can make towers with the set jellies. How high can you build?

♦ Make a 'designer' jelly. Add fruit and berries, 'hundreds and thousands' and other edible cake decorations. Eat your jelly at snack time.

♦ Can you make a savoury jelly? You need some gelatin and small pieces of vegetable — cucumber, cherry tomatoes, celery and peas etc. You can even add cooked pasta shapes.

♦ Make some jellies and when they are set, guess which is heaviest by holding them in your hand. Put them in order from heaviest to lightest. Now weigh them to check your estimates and predictions.

♦ Try making your own jellies from plain gelatin and fruit juices. Add some pieces of fruit to make them taste even better.

♦ Use food colouring to make unusual jelly colours — black, brown or purple.

Materials

Jelly is a really cheap substance to experiment with. Buy bargain versions as long as you don't want the children to eat it, but check for additives and colourings if you do!
There are hundreds of different containers and jelly moulds you can use to set the jellies in. Transparent containers make it easier to see what is going on, and for some experiments where the jelly is not eaten, it doesn't matter if you can't get the jelly out again. Try some of these:

- plastic cups, mugs and bowls
- water bottles with the tops cut off
- yoghurt pots and margarine tubs
- vases and pots for flowers and plants
- liners from jam tarts, chocolates, jelly sweet boxes, food trays
- sand and clay moulds
- biscuit and cake moulds
- commercial jelly moulds

Google images

- jelly
- jelly moulds
- jelly sculpture
- jelly babies

Websites

www.aquarterof.co.uk is a site about sweets where you can look for details of all sorts of sweets, including jelly babies and jelly sharks. This site is good for starting a survey of favourite sweets without buying the actual sweets!

Or try www.historicfood.com for the history of foods and some good pictures of banquets.

www.jellyandicecreamparties.com and www.lakeland.co.uk have pictures of jelly moulds.

Materials, websites, books and other references

Books

Don't Put Your Finger in the Jelly, Nelly; Nick Sharratt; Scholastic

Red Rockets and Rainbow Jelly; Sue Heap

Gargling with Jelly; Brian Patten; Puffin (poetry)

Smelly Jelly, Smelly Feet; Michael Rosen; Walker Books, (poetry)

Juggling a Jug of Jelly; John Foster; OUP (poetry)

Aquarium

Previous experience

Children may have already had an aquarium at home or at school. Experiences may have included :

- experimenting with model fish and plastic plants to make a model aquarium for small world play

- using small world sea life treasures in water play

- watching video and film of underwater stories — real life and fictional

- visiting sea-life centres with their setting or their family

- watching fish and other sea creatures in aquarium shops, garden centres and pet shops.

The responsive adult

In the early stages of working with these materials it is crucial to continue to observe the children. Only by doing this can you set developmentally appropriate challenges and provocations. The ideas listed here are offered as suggestions; the most exciting challenges will arise from children's own interests and motivations, which will only become apparent as you spend time with them, watching and joining them in their play. As you do this, you will be moving between the three interconnecting roles of observer, co-player, extender described below, and will be able to decide what you need to do next to take the learning forward. In three interconnecting roles, the responsive adult will be:

Observer

- observing
- listening
- interpreting

Co-player

- modelling
- playing alongside
- offering suggestions
- responding sensitively
- initiating with care!

Extender

- discussing ideas
- sharing thinking
- modelling new skills
- asking open questions
- being an informed extender
- instigating ideas and thoughts
- supporting children as they make links in learning
- making possibilities evident
- introducing new ideas and resources
- offering challenges and provocations

Offering challenges and provocations

Cheap plastic aquarium plants and aquarium backing, with a plastic tank and some gravel will give children endless hours of play and time to experiment with working underwater.

- Use some plastic plants to make an aquarium in a big plastic container (a washing up bowl or bucket will do if you don't have a tank). Now add some gravel and clean stones.

- Make some fish and other sea creatures to live in your aquarium. They need to be waterproof, so use plastic or other waterproof materials, such as carrier bags, plastic food trays or egg boxes.

- Find an empty cardboard carton and tape it closed. Get an adult to help you cut an opening in one side of the box so you can see inside. Now use the box to make an underwater scene. Paint a background inside the box, put gravel on the base, and make some plants for the aquarium. Now make some fish and hang them on cotton from the roof of the aquarium, so they look as though they are swimming. You could put clear or transparent blue plastic or cling film over the front of the aquarium to look like glass.

- Work with a friend and use books or the internet to find out about fish and other sea creatures. Use some of the images you find to make a book or presentation of what you find out.

- Can you make a model of the fish tank in the dentist's surgery in Finding Nemo? You may need to look at the DVD to remind yourself. Make the fish from card shapes, coloured with felt pens to make them bright and realistic.

- Make a story in pictures and words about a lost baby seahorse. You could use a camera to make some of the pictures.

Ready for more?

◆ Use the internet to find out about Sea Life Centres and Big Aquariums. Email them to see if they will send you more information.

◆ Look up your local pet shop or aquarium shop and see if you can visit to look at tropical fish and other sea creatures. Ask if you can take some photos for an information book or poster for your school.

◆ Work as a class to make a human sized aquarium in the corner of your room. You could hang paper weeds from the ceiling and make rocks with papier mâché. Put some blue fabric on the floor and paint a big background picture with fish, sharks and other sea creatures.

◆ Find out which is the largest sea creature in the world. How big is it? Can you find a picture of it? Now find out about the smallest sea creatures. What do they look like? Try **www. animals.nationalgeographic.co.uk** to find pictures of all sorts of sea creatures.

Materials

You will need some containers to use as aquariums — either plastic fish tanks, big jars or plastic bottles, or cardboard boxes for 'no water' aquarium scenes. Fish tanks and bowls are reasonable prices from aquarium shops, and you can add plants, rocks and stones as well as plastic or real fish. Pound shops are also good places to look for aquarium items.

Google images

- aquarium
- fish sculptures
- fishing
- diver
- crustaceans
- tropical fish
- underwater animals
- river
- seaside
- houseboat

Websites

www.national-aquarium.co.uk with photos, and a tour of the building in Plymouth

www.londonaquarium.co.uk click to the Kids Zone to find facts, and a virtual visit

www.aquariumsonline.eu for biorb aquariums

www.ticket-centre.co.uk/sea-life-centre and click through to UK Sea Life Centres

www.sealifeeurope.com has activity pages

www.bluereefaquarium.co.uk has good fish pictures on the home page

The Deep is the award winning aquarium in Hull which features over 3500 fish and 40 sharks **www.thedeep.co.uk**

www.sheddaquarium.org/oceanarium The site for the Chicago aquarium with views of exhibits.

Materials, websites, books and other references

Books

There are so many suitable stories that we can only suggest a few here:

Rainbow Fish (and other titles by same author), Marcus Pfister; North South Books

Sharks; Jonathan Miller; Usborne

My Trip to the Aquarium; Aliki: Harper Collins

Your First Marine Aquarium; John Tullock, Barron's Educational Series

The Ocean Book; Centre For Marine Conservation; John Wiley

Captain Barnacle's Aquarium; Edward Miller; Harry N Abrahams

1001 Things to Spot in the Sea; Katie Daynes; Usborne

First Encyclopedia of Seas and Oceans; Ben Deane; Usborne

Sea-Life Art and Activities; Judy Press; Williamson Publishing

The Seaside (Curriculum Links); Suzanne Kirk; Scholastic

Seaside Scientist; Mick Manning; Franklin Watts

On the surface

Previous experience

During their time in the Foundation Stage children will have experienced and experimented with floating and sinking activities in:

- free play indoors and outside

- by exploring what happens when objects are put in water

- in the bath at home

- when washing up after cooking and other food activities

- by looking at video and film about boats and water

- in structured, adult-led activities.

The responsive adult

In the early stages of working with these materials it is crucial to continue to observe the children. Only by doing this can you set developmentally appropriate challenges and provocations. The ideas listed here are offered as suggestions; the most exciting challenges will arise from children's own interests and motivations, which will only become apparent as you spend time with them, watching and joining them in their play. As you do this, you will be moving between the three interconnecting roles of observer, co-player, extender described below, and will be able to decide what you need to do next to take the learning forward. In three interconnecting roles, the responsive adult will be:

Observer

- observing
- listening
- interpreting

Co-player

- modelling
- playing alongside
- offering suggestions
- responding sensitively
- initiating with care!

Extender

- discussing ideas
- sharing thinking
- modelling new skills
- asking open questions
- being an informed extender
- instigating ideas and thoughts
- supporting children as they make links in learning
- making possibilities evident
- introducing new ideas and resources
- offering challenges and provocations

Offering challenges and provocations

In these challenges and provocations, we have concentrated on the surface of water. Of course, children will also be involved in the sinking aspect as they work. Much water play in the Foundation Stage may have been child-initiated, and children may need to be helped to focus on a specific challenge.

- Collect 10 waterproof objects from around the room. Now find out if they will float on the surface of water in a bowl or other container. Record what you find out. What happens if you leave the objects in the water for one hour? Does anything change?

- Now can you use what you found out to collect more objects that will float. Do you notice anything similar about the objects that float? Use a camera to help you record what you find.

- Cut some circles from polystyrene or plastic containers. Can you make these float on the top of the water? Try loading the circles with counters. How many can the circle carry before it sinks? Try with different sizes.

- Collect some leaves and float them on the surface of a transparent container of water (such as a plastic aquarium). Now look at the underneath of these flat objects as they float. What can you see? Do different leaves look different? Why could this be?

- Get some cooking oil in a small container. Mix it with a few drops of food colouring if you have some. Now use a dropper or a spoon to drop small amounts of the oil on top of a bowl of water. What happens? Take some photos of your experiment.

- Get some yellow bath ducks (or other bath toys) and find out why they float. Sometimes these toys sink. Why does this happen?

- Experiment with some small water bottles. Can you make them float?

Ready for more?

♦ Continue your experiments with an empty water bottle. Can you make it float upright in the water? Can you make it float upside down?

♦ Find out about water boatmen. How do they stay afloat on the surface of the water? Can you find any other insects that can do this?

♦ Use the internet or a book to find out about marbling. Collect what you need and see if you can do it. Why does the ink stay on top of the water? Why doesn't it mix with the water? When your marbled paper is dry, use it to cover a display board, make a card or cover a book.

♦ Use the internet to find **www.kids-science-experiments.com** and try some of these experiments: Swimming Fish, Speedboat Matchsticks, Run Away Pepper and Bubbles. They are in the 'surface tension' section. When you have tried some of the experiments, show them to your friends and explain how they work (it tells you on the website!)

♦ Find some different sorts of seeds and test them to see if they float or sink. Use a camera to record your experiments. Why do you think some seeds float?

♦ Buy a water hyacinth or a water lily plant from a garden centre and keep it in a bucket. How does it live? You could add a goldfish to your pond as long as you remember to feed it!

Materials

Simple floating experiments can be done with a range of free materials such as:

- sticks, leaves, seeds and seed pods
- feathers, coins, pieces of bark, stones and pebbles
- offcuts of plywood or pieces of driftwood
- plastic, card and paper
- small world animals and people, construction toy pieces and marbles

Google Images

- water creatures
- water insects
- water boatman
- swans
- colour changing ducks

Websites

One of the very best sites for teachers and children is **www.kathimitchell.com** where you can click through to science experiments and other education and information sites across the world - you could spend a whole term here.

Other sites include **www.show.me.uk** is a museum and information site for children with links to many UK museums and galleries. A site with simple science experiments for young children is **www.kids-science-experiments.com** where you can find experiments on surface tension such as 'fish', 'speedboat matchsticks', 'run away pepper' and 'bubbles'. Loads of easy experiments without complicated resources.

Materials, websites, books and other references

Books

Down in the Cool of the Pool; Tony Mitton; Orchard Books

Rory and his Rock Pool Adventure; Andrew Wolffe; Kepple Publishing

In One Tidepool; Anthony Fredericks; Dawn Publications

In the Pond; Ruth Wickins; Mercury Junior

Pond and River; Steve Parker; Dorling Kindersley

What's in The Pond; Anne Hunter; Houghton Mifflin

Creating a Wildlife Pond; Dave Bevan; Ringpress Books

Tadpoles and Frogs; Anna Milbourne; Usborne

Pond Dipping; Alison Hawes; Collins

Pond and River; Steve Parker; DK

Song of the Water Boatman; Joyce Sidman; Houghton Mifflin (Non fiction book award winner)

The Web at Dragonfly Pond; Brian Ellis; Dawn Publications

Turtle Splash; Cathryn Falwell; Greenwillow Books

Christmas at Long Pond; William T George; HarperTrophy

Waterproofing

Previous experience

Children will have had experience of waterproofing and protection from water in activities such as:

- during water play;
- when watering plants in the garden;
- when discussing protective clothing to wear out of doors and on visits;
- talking about the purpose of wearing aprons when washing things out of doors or using wet and messy materials indoors;
- making sure surfaces and objects are protected from water by covering them with waterproof materials.

The responsive adult

In the early stages of working with these materials it is crucial to continue to observe the children. Only by doing this can you set developmentally appropriate challenges and provocations. The ideas listed here are offered as suggestions; the most exciting challenges will arise from children's own interests and motivations, which will only become apparent as you spend time with them, watching and joining them in their play. As you do this, you will be moving between the three interconnecting roles of observer, co-player, extender described below, and will be able to decide what you need to do next to take the learning forward. In three interconnecting roles, the responsive adult will be:

Observer

- observing
- listening
- interpreting

Co-player

- modelling
- playing alongside
- offering suggestions
- responding sensitively
- initiating with care!

Extender

- discussing ideas
- sharing thinking
- modelling new skills
- asking open questions
- being an informed extender
- instigating ideas and thoughts
- supporting children as they make links in learning
- making possibilities evident
- introducing new ideas and resources
- offering challenges and provocations

Offering challenges and provocations

Provide a wide range of materials for children to test and explore. Let them use these in free exploration before setting challenges.

- Collect some materials to test for waterproofness. Find a fair way of testing each material. Record your findings in a graph or chart, so it is easy to see which materials are waterproof and which are not waterproof.

- Design and make some waterproof clothes for a doll, soft toy or puppet.

- Put a small toy or teddy in a cardboard box. Now make the box completely waterproof. Leave it submerged in water overnight to test how well it works — don't forget to rescue the toy and dry it out!

- Try the same experiment with different containers and different methods of waterproofing. Put porridge oats, Smarties or biscuits in the containers before waterproofing them.

- Waterproof a cardboard box and fill it full of 'treasure'. Submerge your treasure chest in water and see what happens.

- Collect some plastic carrier bags and use these to waterproof something. Use just the carrier bags, no tape, glue or string! Are some bags better than others? Is it possible to make something waterproof using ONLY plastic bags?

- Find some waterproof gloves and footwear. What makes them special? Why are they waterproof? Can you design other ways of keeping your feet and hands dry? Try making what you have designed and trying it out.

- Get some thin plastic sheeting (plastic dustsheets are cheap and easy to use). Can you make a waterproof shelter with plastic sheeting and canes or sticks?

Ready for more?

- ♦ Find out how you could use wax to make something waterproof. Candles or crayons are good starting points.

- ♦ Look at varnishes. How do they work to protect things from water. Use the internet to find out how they work and all the different sorts you can buy. You could try some water-based varnishes, or varnish things with PVA glue. What are the problems with water-based varnish?

- ♦ Can you make small objects (Lego pieces, marbles or pasta shapes) completely waterproofed by enclosing them in Plasticene or Blutack? Test what you have done.

- ♦ Collect some natural materials (feathers, leaves, bark, shells, pebbles etc). Use coloured water and a dropper to find out which ones are waterproof.

- ♦ Make a small pond outside. Find out how to stop the pond leaking. Explore 'pond liners' on the internet, and try to find out how people made ponds before there were pond liners. If possible, look at natural ponds and puddles for clues.

- ♦ Use a range of plastic materials — bin bags, carrier bags, plastic sheeting — to make your own waterproof clothing. Test it in the rain or with sprays.

- ♦ Explore umbrellas - how they work and try making one yourself from sticks and plastic or waterproof fabric.

Materials

Recycled materials are free, so make sure the children have plenty of choice and can get the things they want to use as they work with waterproofing experiments. Why not put a notice up inviting offers of *clean* recycled materials such as:

- ■ plastic bottles and tops, containers, cups, tubs and pots

- ■ old waterproof clothing such as raincoats, boots and leggings

Collect some cheap items for experiments:

- ■ umbrellas (adult and children's)

- ■ watering cans and sprays

- ■ duct and masking tapes (from 'Pound' shops)

- ■ string, wool, soft wire, cord and rope

- ■ scraps of fabric, plastic bags, plastic sheeting, bubble wrap to make trial clothes and structures

It's important to give children plenty of time to work on their projects and to find some way of protecting unfinished projects and tests, indoors and outside, particularly if you are expecting them to photograph the experiments for a book or presentation.

Google Images

To inspire their work try putting words such as:

- • tent
- • tarpaulin
- • shelter
- • bubble wrap
- • souwester
- • oilskin
- • water collector

Materials, websites, books and other references

Websites

www.allplas.co.uk for plastic covers, tarpaulins, bubble-wrap, greenhouse insulation, polythene sheeting and much more.

At www.showplace.uk.com the Gallery has lots of examples of weatherproof structures.

Or try Olympic Games sites for buildings with sliding roofs and waterproof structures - www.london2012.com and www.olympics.org.uk

Books

Wild About the Weather; 50 wet activities; Ed Brotak; Lark Books;

Tell Me Why Rain is Wet; Shirley Willis; Book House

Wet World; Norma Simon; Candlewick Press

Plastic Raincoat (Our Clothes); Wayne Jackman; Hodder

The Tent; Dorothy Mills; Bookman Publishing

Camp Out!; Lynne Brunelle; Workman Publishing

Plastic; Henry Pluckrose; Franklin Watts

Working with Materials; C Chapman; Collins

How we Use Plastic; Chris Oxlade; Raintree

Plastic (Science Explorers); Nicola Edwards; A & C Black

NC KS1 Programme of Study (revised Framework objectives)   Literacy - Year 1

Literacy 1 Speaking	<ul><li>Retell stories, ordering events using story language</li><li>Tell stories and describe incidents from their own experience in an audible voice.</li><li>Interpret a text by reading aloud with some variety in pace and emphasis</li><li>Experiment with and build new stores of words to communicate in different contexts.</li></ul>	**Literacy 6** Word structure and spelling	<ul><li>Spell new words using phonics as the prime approach</li><li>Segment sounds into their constituent phonemes in order to spell them correctly. Children move from spelling simple CVC words to longer words that include common diagraphs & adjacent consonants such as 'brush', 'crunch'</li><li>Recognise and use alternative ways of spelling the graphemes already taught, for example that the /ae/ sound can be spelt with 'ai', 'ay' or 'a-e'; that the /ee/ sound can also be spelt as 'ea' and 'e'; & begin to know which words contain which spelling alternatives</li><li>Use knowledge of common inflections in spelling, such as plurals, -ly, -er</li><li>Read and spell phonically decodable two and three syllable words.</li></ul>	**Literacy 8** Engaging and responding to text	<ul><li>Select books for personal reading and give reasons for choices</li><li>Visualise and comment on events, characters and ideas, making imaginative links to their own experiences</li><li>Distinguish fiction and nonfiction texts and the different purposes for reading them.</li></ul>
Literacy 2 Listening and responding	<ul><li>Listen with sustained concentration, building new stores of words in different contexts</li><li>Listen to tapes or video and express views about how a story or information has been presented</li><li>Listen to and follow instructions accurately, asking for help and clarification if necessary.</li></ul>			**Literacy 9** Creating and shaping texts	<ul><li>Independently choose what to write about, plan and follow it through</li><li>Use key features of narrative in their own writing</li><li>Convey information and ideas in simple non-narrative forms</li><li>Find and use new and interesting words and phrases, including story language</li><li>Create short simple texts on paper and on screen that combine words with images (and sounds).</li></ul>
Literacy 3 Group discussion & interaction	<ul><li>Take turns to speak, listen to others' suggestions and talk about what they are going to do</li><li>Ask and answer questions, make relevant contributions, offer suggestions and take turns</li><li>Explain their views to others in a small group, decide how to report the group's views to the class.</li></ul>	**Literacy 7** Understanding and interpreting texts	<ul><li>Identify the main events and characters in stories, and find specific information in simple texts</li><li>Use syntax and context when reading for meaning</li><li>Make predictions showing an understanding of ideas, events and characters</li><li>Recognise the main elements that shape different texts</li><li>Explore the effect of patterns of language and repeated words and phrases.</li></ul>	**Literacy 10** Text structure and organisation	<ul><li>Write chronological and non-chronological texts using simple structures</li><li>Group written sentences together in chunks of meaning or subject.</li></ul>
Literacy 4 Drama	<ul><li>Explore familiar themes and characters through improvisation and role-play</li><li>Act out their own and well-known stories, using voices for characters</li><li>Discuss why they like a performance.</li></ul>			**Literacy 11** Sentence structure and punctuation	<ul><li>Compose and write simple sentences independently to communicate meaning</li><li>Use capital letters and full stops when punctuating simple sentences.</li></ul>
Literacy 5 Word recognition, coding and decoding	<ul><li>Recognise and use alternative ways of pronouncing the graphemes already taught, for example, that the grapheme 'g' is pronounced differently in 'get' and 'gem'; the grapheme 'ow' is pronounced differently in 'how' and 'show'</li><li>Recognise and use alternative ways of spelling the phonemes already taught, for example 'ae" can be spelt with 'ai', 'ay' or 'a-e'; begin to know which words contain which spelling alternatives</li><li>Identify the constituent parts of two-syllable and three-syllable words to support the application of phonic knowledge and skills. Recognise automatically an increasing number of familiar high frequency words</li></ul>		<ul><li>Apply phonic knowledge and skills as the prime approach to reading and spelling unfamiliar words that are not completely decodable</li><li>Read more challenging texts which can be decoded using their acquired phonic knowledge and skills; automatic recognition of high frequency words. Read and spell phonically decodable two-syllable and three-syllable words.</li></ul>	**Literacy 12** Presentation	<ul><li>Write most letters, correctly formed and orientated, using a comfortable and efficient pencil grip</li><li>Write with spaces between words accurately</li><li>Use the space bar and keyboard to type their name and simple texts.</li></ul>

KS1 Programme of Study (revised Framework objectives) Literacy - Year 2

Literacy 1 **Speaking**	
	• Speak with clarity and use appropriate intonation when reading and reciting texts
	• Tell real and imagined stories using the conventions of familiar story language
	• Explain ideas and processes using imaginative and adventurous vocabulary and nonverbal gestures to support communication

Literacy 2 **Listening and responding**	
	• Listen to others in class, ask relevant questions and follow instructions
	• Listen to talk by an adult, remember some specific points and identify what they have learned
	• Respond to presentations by describing characters, repeating some highlight and commenting constructively

Literacy 3 **Group discussion and interaction**	
	• Ensure that everyone contributes, allocate tasks, and consider alternatives and reach agreement
	• Work effectively in groups by ensuring that each group member takes a turn challenging, supporting and moving on
	• Listen to each other's views and preferences, agree the next steps to take and identify contributions by each group member

Literacy 4 **Drama**	
	• Adopt appropriate roles in small or large groups and consider alternative courses of action
	• Present part of traditional stories, their own stories or work drawn from different parts of the curriculum for members of their own class
	• Consider how mood and atmosphere are created in live or recorded performance

Literacy 5 **Word recognition, coding and decoding**	
	• Read independently and with increasing fluency longer and less familiar texts
	• Spell with increasing accuracy and confidence, drawing on word recognition and knowledge of word structure, and spelling patterns
	• Know how to tackle unfamiliar words that are not completely decodable
	• Read and spell less common alternative graphemes including trigraphs
	• Read high and medium frequency words independently and automatically

Literacy 6 **Word structure and spelling**	
	• Spell with increasing accuracy and confidence, drawing on word recognition and knowledge of word structure, and spelling patterns including common inflections and use of double letters
	• Read and spell less common alternative graphemes including trigraphs

Literacy 7 **Understanding and interpreting texts**	
	• Draw together ideas and information from across a whole text, using simple signposts in the text
	• Give reasons why things happen or characters change
	• Explain organisational features of texts, including alphabetical order, layout, diagrams etc
	• Use syntax and context to build their store of vocabulary when reading
	• Explore how particular words are used, including words and expressions with similar meanings

Literacy 8 **Engaging and responding to text**	
	• Read whole books on their own, choosing and justifying selections
	• Engage with books through exploring and enacting interpretations
	• Explain their reactions to texts, commenting on important aspects

Literacy 9 **Creating and shaping texts**	
	• Draw on knowledge and experience of texts in deciding and planning what and how to write
	• Sustain form in narrative, including use of person and time
	• Maintain consistency in non- narrative, including purpose and tense
	• Make adventurous word and language choices appropriate to the style and purpose of the text
	• Select from different presentational features to suit particular writing purposes on paper and on screen

Literacy 10 **Text structure and organisation**	
	• Use planning to establish clear sections for writing
	• Use appropriate language to make sections hang together

Literacy 11 **Sentence structure and punctuation**	
	• Write simple and compound sentences and begin to use subordination in relation to time and reason
	• Compose sentences using tense consistently (present and past)
	• Use question marks, and use commas to separate items in a list

Literacy 12 **Presentation**	
	• Write legibly, using upper and lower case letters appropriately within words, and observing correct spacing within and between words
	• Form and use the four basic handwriting joins
	• Word process short narrative and non- narrative texts

Mathematics 1 Using and applying maths	• Solve problems involving counting, adding, subtracting, doubling or halving in the context of numbers, measures or money, for example to 'pay' and 'give change' • Describe a puzzle or problem using numbers, practical materials and diagrams; use these to solve the problem and set the solution in the original context • Answer a question by selecting and using suitable equipment, and sorting information, shapes or objects; display results using tables and pictures • Describe simple patterns and relationships involving numbers or shapes; decide whether examples satisfy given conditions • Describe ways of solving puzzles and problems, explaining choices and decisions orally or using pictures	**Mathematics 4** Calculating	• Relate addition to counting on; recognise that addition can be done in any order; use practical and informal written methods to support the addition of a one-digit number or a multiple of 10 to a one-digit or two- digit number • Understand subtraction as 'take away' and find a 'difference' by counting up; use practical and informal written methods to support the subtraction of a one-digit number from a one-digit or two digit number and a multiple of 10 from a two- digit number • Solve practical problems that involve combining groups of 2, 5 or 10, or sharing into equal groups • Use the vocabulary related to addition and subtraction and symbols to describe and record addition and subtraction number sentences
Mathematics 2 Counting and understanding numbers	• Count reliably at least 20 objects, recognising that when rearranged the number of objects stays the same; estimate a number of objects that can be checked by counting • Compare and order numbers, using the related vocabulary; use the equals (=) sign • Read and write numerals from 0 to 20, then beyond; use knowledge of place value to position these numbers on a number track and number line • Say the number that is 1 more or less than any given number, and 10 more or less for multiples of 10 • Use the vocabulary of halves and quarters in context	**Mathematics 5** Understanding shape	• Visualise and name common 2-D shapes and 3-D solids and describe their features; use them to make patterns, pictures and models • Identify objects that turn about a point (e.g. scissors) or about a line (e.g. a door); recognise and make whole, half and quarter turns • Visualise and use everyday language to describe the position of objects and direction and distance when moving them, for example when placing or moving objects on a game board
		Mathematics 6 Measuring	• Estimate, measure, weigh and compare objects, choosing and using suitable uniform non-standard or standard units and measuring instruments (e.g. a lever balance, metre stick or measuring jug) • Use vocabulary related to time; order days of the week and months; read the time to the hour and half hour
Mathematics 3 Knowing and using number facts	• Derive and recall all pairs of numbers with a total of 10 and addition facts for totals to at least 5; work out the corresponding subtraction facts • Count on or back in ones, twos, fives and tens and use this knowledge to derive the multiples of 2, 5 and 10 to the tenth multiple • Recall the doubles of all numbers to at least 10	**Mathematics 7** Handling data	• Answer a question by recording information in lists and tables; present outcomes using practical resources, pictures, block graphs or pictograms • Use diagrams to sort objects into groups according to a given criterion; suggest a different criterion for grouping the same objects

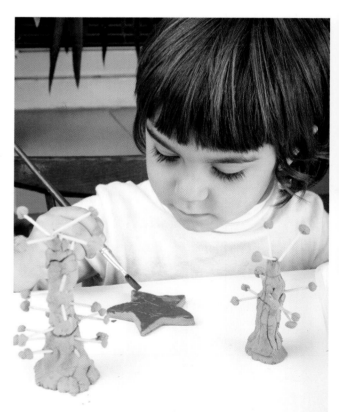

Mathematics 1
Using and applying maths

- Solve problems involving addition, subtraction, multiplication or division in contexts of numbers, measures or pounds and pence
- Identify and record the information or calculation needed to solve a puzzle or problem; carry out the steps or calculations and check the solution in the context of the problem
- Follow a line of enquiry; answer questions by choosing and using suitable equipment and selecting, organising and presenting information in lists, tables and simple diagrams
- Describe patterns and relationships involving numbers or shapes, make predictions and test these with examples
- Present solutions to puzzles and problems in an organised way; explain decisions, methods and results in pictorial, spoken or written form, using mathematical language and number sentences

Mathematics 2
Counting and understanding numbers

- Read and write two-digit and three-digit numbers in figures and words; describe and extend number sequences and recognise odd and even numbers
- Count up to 100 objects by grouping them and counting in tens, fives or twos; explain what each digit in a two-digit number represents, including numbers where 0 is a place holder; partition two-digit numbers in different ways, including into multiples of 10 and 1
- Order two-digit numbers and position them on a number line; use the greater than (>) and less than (<) signs
- Estimate a number of objects; round two-digit numbers to the nearest 10
- Find one half, one quarter and three quarters of shapes and sets of objects

Mathematics 3
Knowing and using number facts

- Derive and recall all addition and subtraction facts for each number to at least 10, all pairs with totals to 20 and all pairs of multiples of 10 with totals up to 100
- Understand that halving is the inverse of doubling and derive and recall doubles of all numbers to 20, and the corresponding halves
- Derive and recall multiplication facts for the 2, 5 and 10 times-tables and the related division facts; recognise multiples of 2, 5 and 10
- Use knowledge of number facts and operations to estimate and check answers to calculations

Mathematics 4
Calculating

- Add or subtract mentally a one-digit number or a multiple of 10 to or from any two-digit number; use practical and informal written methods to add and subtract two-digit numbers
- Understand that subtraction is the inverse of addition and vice versa; use this to derive and record related addition and subtraction number sentences
- Represent repeated addition and arrays as multiplication, and sharing and repeated subtraction (grouping) as division; use practical and informal written methods and related vocabulary to support multiplication and division, including calculations with remainders
- Use the symbols $+$, $-$, $?$, $\div$ and $=$ to record and interpret number sentences involving all four operations; calculate the value of an unknown in a number sentence (e.g. $\square \div 2 = 60$, $30 - \square = 24$).

Mathematics 5
Understanding shape

- Visualise common 2-D shapes and 3-D solids; identify shapes from pictures of them in different positions and orientations; sort, make and describe shapes, referring to their properties
- Identify reflective symmetry in patterns and 2-D shapes and draw lines of symmetry in shapes
- Follow and give instructions involving position, direction and movement
- Recognise and use whole, half and quarter turns, both clockwise and anticlockwise; know that a right angle represents a quarter turn

Mathematics 6
Measuring

- Estimate, compare & measure lengths, weights and capacities, choosing & using standard units (m, cm, kg, litre) & suitable measuring instruments
- Read the numbered divisions on a scale, and interpret the divisions between them (e.g. on a scale from 0 to 25 with intervals of 1 shown but only the divisions 0, 5, 10, 15 and 20 numbered); use a ruler to draw and measure lines to the nearest centimetre
- Use units of time (seconds, minutes, hours, days) and know the relationships between them; read the time to the quarter hour; identify time intervals, including those that cross the hour

Mathematics 7
Handling data

- Answer a question by collecting and recording data in lists and tables; represent the data as block graphs or pictograms to show results; use ICT to organise and present data
- Use lists, tables and diagrams to sort objects; explain choices using appropriate language, including 'not'

KS1 Programme of Study for Key Stage 1: Science

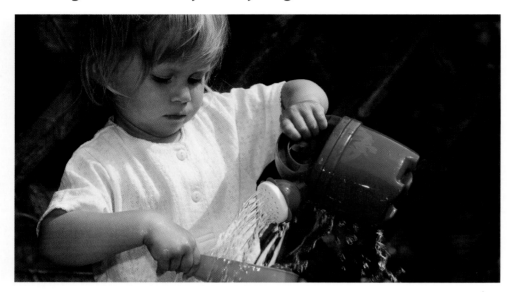

SC1 Scientific enquiry

Sc 1.1	1.1a	1.1b	1.1c	1.1d
Planning	Ask questions 'How?', 'Why?', 'What if?' and decide how they might find answers to them	Use first-hand experience and simple information sources to answer questions	Think about what might happen before deciding what to do	Recognise when a test or comparison is unfair

Sc 1.2	1.2a	1.2b	1.2c	1.2d
Ideas and evidence, collecting evidence	Follow simple instructions to control the risks to themselves and to others	Explore using the senses of sight, hearing, smell, touch and taste as appropriate. Make and record observations and measurements	Communicate what happened in a variety of ways including using ICT	

Sc 1.3	1.3a	1.3b	1.3c	1.3d
Comparing evidence	Make simple comparisons (eg, hand span, shoe size) and identify simple patterns or associations, and try to explain it, drawing on their knowledge and understanding	Compare what happened with what they expected would happen and try to explain it. Draw on their knowledge and understanding	Review their work and explain what they did to others	

SC2 Life processes and living things

Sc 2.1	2.1a	2.1b	2.1c	2.1d
Life processes	Differences between things that are living and things that have never been alive	That animals, including humans, move, feed, grow, use their senses and reproduce	Relate life processes to animals and plants found in the local environment	

Sc 2.2	2.2a	2.2b	2.2c	2.2d
Ideas and evidence, collecting evidence	Recognise and compare the main external parts of the bodies of humans and other animals	That humans and other animals need food and water to stay alive	That taking exercise and eating the right types and amounts of food help humans to keep healthy	About the role of drugs as medicines
	2.2e	**2.2f**	**2.2g**	
	How to treat animals with care and sensitivity	That humans and other animals can produce off-spring and these off-spring grow into adults	About the senses that enable humans and other animals to be aware of the world around them	

Sc 2.3	2.3a	2.3b	2.3c	2.3d
Green plants	Recognise that plants need light and water to grow	To recognise and name the leaf, flowers, stem and root of flowering plants	That seeds grow into flowering plants	

Sc 2.4	2.4a	2.4b		
Variation and classification	Recognise similarities and differences between themselves and others, and to treat others with sensitivity	Group living things according to observable similarities and differences		

Sc 2.5	2.5a	2.5b	2.5c
Living things in their environment	Find out about the different kinds of plants and animals in the local environment	Identify similarities & differences between local environments & ways in which these affect animals & plants that are found there	Care for the environment

SC3 Materials and their properties

Sc 3.1	3.1a	3.1b	3.1c	3.1d
Grouping materials	Use their senses to explore and recognise the similarities and differences between materials	Sort objects into groups on the basis of their properties: texture, float, hardness and transparency and whether they are magnetic or non-magnetic	Recognise and name common types of material and recognise that some of them are found naturally	Find out about the uses of a variety of materials and how these are chosen for specific uses on the basis of their simple properties
Sc 3.2	**3.2a**	**3.2b**		
Changing materials	Find out how the shapes of objects made from some materials can be changed by some processes including squashing, bending, twisting and stretching	Explore and describe the way some everyday materials, e.g. water, chocolate, bread and clay, change when they are heated or cooled		

SC4 Physical processes

Sc 4.1	4.1a	4.1b	4.1c	4.1d
Electricity	About everyday appliances that use electricity	Simple series circuits involving batteries, wires, bulbs and other components e.g. buzzers	How a switch can be used to break a circuit	Recognise when a test or comparison is unfair
Sc 4.2	**4.2a**	**4.2b**	**4.2c**	
Forces and motion	Find out about and describe the movement of familiar things e.g. cars going faster, slowing down, changing direction	That both pushes and pulls are examples of forces	To recognise that when things speed up, slow down, or change direction there is a cause	
Sc 4.3	**4.3a**	**4.3b**	**4.3c**	**4.3d**
Light and sound	Identify different light sources including the sun	That darkness is the absence of light	That there are many kinds of sound and sources of sound	That sounds travel away from sources, getting fainter as they do so, and that they are heard

KS1 Programmes of Study

Design and Technology

D&T 1	1a	1b	1c	1d	1e
Developing, planning and communicating ideas	Generate ideas by drawing on their own and other people's experiences	Develop ideas by hoping materials and putting together components	Talk about their ideas	Plan by suggesting what to do next as their ideas develop	Communicate ideas using a variety of materials including drawing and making moulds
D&T 2	**2a**	**2b**	**2c**	**2d**	**2e**
Working with tools, equipment and materials	Explore sensory qualities of materials	Measure, mark out, cut and shape	Assemble, join and combine materials	Use simple finishing techniques	Follow safe procedures
D&T 3	**3a**	**3b**			
Evaluating processes and products	Talk about their ideas	Identify improvements			
D&T 4	**4a**	**4b**			
Knowledge & understanding of materials and components	Working characteristics of materials	How mechanisms can be used			
D&T 5	**5a**	**5b**	**5c**		
Breadth of study	Focused practical tasks	Design and make assignments	Investigate and evaluate products		

History

H 1	1a	1b	1c
Chronological understanding	Place events and objects in chronological order	Use common words and phrases relating to the passing of time e.g. before, after, a long time ago and past	Retrieve information that has been stored
H 2	**2a**	**2b**	
Knowledge & understanding of events people and changes	Recognise why people did things, why events happened and what happened as a result	Identify differences between ways of life at different times	
H 3	**3a**		
Historical interpretation	Identify different ways in which the past is represented		
H 4	**4a**	**4b**	
Historical enquiry	Find out about the past from a range of sources of information	Ask and answer questions about the past	
H 5	**5a**		
Organisation and communication	Select from their knowledge of history and communicate it in a variety of ways		
H 6	**6a**	**6b**	**6c**	**6d**
Breadth of study	Changes in their own lives and the way of life of their family or others around them	The way of life of people in the more distant past who lived in the local area or elsewhere in Britain	The lives of significant men, women or children	Past events from the history of Britain and the wider world

Geography

G 1.1	1.1a	1.1b	1.1c	1.1d	
Geographical enquiry	Ask geographical questions	Observe and record	Express their own views about people, places, and environments	Communicate in different ways	
G 1.2	**1.2a**	**1.2b**	**1.2c**	**1.2d**	
Geographical skills	Use geographical vocabulary	Use fieldwork skills	Use globes, maps and plans at a range of scales	Use secondary sources of information	
G 2	**2a**	**2b**	**2c**	**2d**	**2e**
Knowledge and understanding of places	Identify and describe what places are like	Identify and describe what places are	Recognise how places become they way they are & how they are changing	Recognise how places compare with other places	Recognise how places are linked to other places in the world
G 3	**3a**	**3b**	**3c**	**3d**	
Knowledge & understanding of patterns & processes	Make observations about where things are located	Recognise changes in physical & human features			
G 4	**4a**	**4b**			
Knowledge & understanding of environment	Recognise changes in the environment	Recognise how the environment may be improved & sustained			
G 5	**5a**	**5b**	**5c**	**5d**	
Breadth of study	The locality of the school	A contrasting locality in the UK or overseas	Study at a local scale	Carry out fieldwork investigations outside the classroom	

ICT

ICT 1.1	1.1a	1.1b	1.1c	1.1d
Finding things out	Gather information from a variety of sources	Enter and store information in a variety of forms	Retrieve information that has been stored	
ICT 1.2	**1.2a**	**1.2b**	**1.2c**	**1.2d**
Developing ideas and making things happen	Use text, tables, images and sound to develop their ideas	Select from and add to information thay have rerieved for particular purposes	Plan and give instructions to make things happen	Try things out and explore what happens in real and imaginary instructions
ICT 2	**2a**	**2b**		
Exchanging and sharing information	Share their ideas by presenting information in a variety of forms	Present their completed work effectively		

Physical Education

PE 1	1a	1b	
Aquiring and developing skills	Explore basic skills, actions and ideas with increasing understanding	Remember and repeat simple skills & actions with increasing control	
PE 2	**2a**	**2b**	**2c**
Selecting and applying skills, tactics and compositional ideas	Explore how to choose and apply skills and actions in sequence & in combination	Vary the way they perform skills by using simple tactics and movement phrases	Apply rules and conventions for different activities
PE 3	**3a**	**3b**	**3c**
Evaluating and improving performance	Describe what they have done	Observe, describe & copy what others have done	Use what they have learnt to improve the quality and control of their work
PE 4	**4a**	**4b**	
Knowledge and understanding of fitness and health	How important it is to be active	Recognise and describe how their bodies feel during different activities	
PE 5	**5a**	**5b**	**5c**
Breadth of study	Dance	Games	Gymnastics

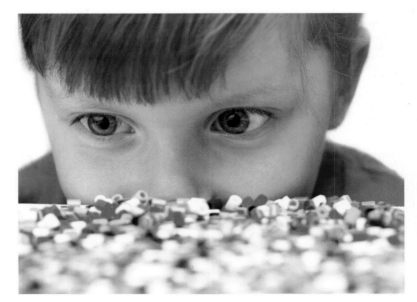

Art and Design

A&D 1	1a	1b		
Exploring and developing ideas	Record from first hand observation, experience & imagination	Ask and answer questions about the starting points for their work		
A&D 2	**2a**	**2b**	**2c**	
Investigating and making art, craft and design	Investigate the possibilities of materials and processes	Try out tools and techniques and apply these	Represent observations, ideas and feelings	
A&D 3	**3a**	**3b**		
Evaluating and developing work	Review what they and others have done	Identify what they might change		
A&D 4	**4a**	**4b**	**4c**	
Knowledge and understanding of materials and components	Visual and tactile elements	Materials and processes used in making art, craft and design	Differences and similarities in the work of artists, craftspeople and designers	
A&D 5	**5a**	**5b**	**5c**	**5d**
Breadth of study	Exploring a range of starting points	Working on their own and collaborating with others	Using a range of materials and processes	Investigating different types of art, craft and design

Music

M 1	1a	1b	1c
Performing skills	Use their voices expressively by singing songs, chants, rhymes	Play tuned and untuned instruments	Rehearse and perform with others
M 2	**2a**	**2b**	
Composing skills	Create musical patterns	Explore, choose and organise sounds and musical ideas	
M 3	**3a**	**3b**	
Responding and reviewing — appraising skills	Explore and express their ideas and feelings about music	Make improvements to their own work	
M 4	**4a**	**4b**	**4c**
Responding and reviewing — listening skills	Listen with concentration and internalise & recall sounds	How combined musical elements can be organised	How sounds can be made in different ways
M 5	**5a**	**5b**	**5c** 5d
Breadth of study	A range of musical activities	Responding to a range of starting points	Working on their own, in groups and as a class — A range of live and recorded music

PSHE

PSHE 1	1a	1b	1c	1d	1e			
Developing confidence & responsibility & making the most of their abilities	Recognise their likes and dislikes, what is fair and unfair, what is right and wrong	Share their opinions on things that matter to them and their views	Recognise, name and deal with their feelings in a positive way	Think about themselves, learn from their experiences and recognise what they are good at	How to set simple goals			
PSHE 2	**2a**	**2b**	**2c**	**2d**	**2e**	**2f**	**2g**	
Preparing to play an active role as citizens	Take part in discussions with one other person and the whole class	Take part in a simple debate about topical issues	Recognise choices they make, and the difference between right and wrong	Realise that people and other living things have needs, and that they have responsibilities to meet them	That they belong to various groups and communities, such as a family	What improves and harms their local, natural & built environments	Contribute to the life of the class and school	Realise that money comes from different sources
PSHE 3	**3a**	**3b**	**3c**	**3d**	**3e**	**3f**	**3g**	
Developing a healthier lifestyle	Make simple choices that improve their health and wellbeing	Maintain personal hygiene	How some diseases spread and can be controlled	About the process of growing from young to old and how people's needs change	Name the main parts of the body	That household products and medicines can be harmful	Rules for, and ways of, keeping safe, basic road safety	
PSHE 4	**4a**	**4b**	**4c**	**4d**	**4e**			
Developing good relationships and respecting differences	Recognise how their behaviour affects other people	Listen to other people and play and work co-operatively	Identify and respect differences and similarities between people	That family and friends should care for each other	That there are different types of teasing and bullying, that bullying is wrong			

PSHE: non-statutory guidance